CW01464565

Weight Loss with Hypnosis

The Ultimate Practitioner's Guide

Kelley T. Woods

Copyright © 2017 Kelley T. Woods All Rights Reserved

Cover Design by Louisa Persephone Firethorne lungraphics.com

No part of this book may be reproduced or transmitted in any form whatsoever, electronic or mechanical including photocopying, recording or by any informational storage or retrieval system without the expressed written, dated and signed permission of the author. Permission is granted to use the scripts offered, in spoken or recorded form, for personal use or within private practice, but not otherwise for commercial gain.

Disclaimer: *The author of this book does not analyze, prescribe or diagnose any mental or medical illness. Information contained and shared here is meant to be used within the reader's individual scope of practice.*

TABLE OF CONTENTS

Introduction

Welcome! You are most likely reading this book because you are either a hypnosis practitioner or another type of wellness provider, or perhaps you are personally interested in the many ways that hypnosis can help in the area of weight loss.

During my fifteen years of clinical hypnosis practice, I have helped many people gain control over their weight challenges. Some time ago, I became aware of a bit of a void in the hypnosis instructional world when it comes to addressing weight issues, which is ironic since this is an area in which our clients most frequently need help.

It's undeniable that obesity and its related health problems is one of the biggest challenges that not only Western nations, but many developing countries are facing. The Journal of Health Economics attributes over $200 billion annually to U.S. obesity-related medical costs.

As the Western S.A.D. (Standard American Diet) of processed, high fat, sodium and sugar-laden food and drink spreads to other countries, rates of heart disease, diabetes and other life-threatening problems are increasing.

The diet industry has been taking overweight people for a ride for decades (over $2 billion worth in 2015 alone in the U.S.A.) – most of my clients have tried several fad diets and other programs that always fail them, leaving them feeling even more discouraged.

Hypnosis presents a refreshing approach that can safely serve on its own but also wonderfully augments any medically-prescribed regime. Even for people who opt for bariatric surgery intervention, hypnosis can be the key element that provides permanent results.

Within this comprehensive guide, I share not only my own, unique point of view along with proven approaches and techniques but also, with permission, some favorites from my respected colleagues. "Patter Boxes" contain proven effective language patterns to enhance your own hypnotic skillset and an appendix offers helpful forms, in addition to sample recording scripts.

Along with some of my unique ideas, I have placed my personal spin on the ideas of others and encourage you to do the same. When I am using patter or even a script that someone else has created, I almost feel as if I am channeling that person. This is a wonderful perspective because it not only expands my abilities, it reminds me that I'm not in this alone.

And neither are you. Simply by reading and incorporating the information and approaches in this guide, you are inviting me to be part of the healing journey with your clients, while you add to your own skillset. So, I thank you for that and invite you to step into my hypnotic world as we explore the many fascinating ways we can help people get healthier and happier!

Chapter One   Preparation

Who Are You?

Before you offer help to others, it's a good idea to assess and determine your perspective, your qualifications and your mode of practice. Everyone is different, as that ironic statement points out, and that not only includes the variety of clients who come to you for help, it includes yourself.

Spend some time to consider your personal beliefs about weight, nutrition, eating, etc. You may have some extensive training in the area of nutrition or you may have more of a laymen's level of knowledge about healthy eating. Wherever you are, please be sure to stay within your scope of education and practice. Personally, I have found it best to refrain from recommending any particular style of eating to my clients, beyond reducing the consumption of processed, refined food and adding more whole foods in proper amounts.

I have worked with clients who are convinced a Paleo approach is right for them while some stick to a plant-based diet, and others who swear by a Weight Watchers approach, and some who use Medifast Liquid Meal Replacement, Jenny Craig meals and a number of other, really whacko diets. Many of my clients, despite having obsessed about food for years, have limited nutritional knowledge and are, in fact, overwhelmed by the confusing array of current recommendations.

While it is pretty evident that diets in the long run don't support lasting results and can even be harmful to a person's health, most people are still stuck in some kind of diet mentality when they come to us. They still believe that they need to suffer in order to lose weight. It's our job to free them from that senseless struggle and help them cultivate a more intelligent, viable relationship with food.

I encourage my clients to focus less on the actual weight loss, which will arrive on its own time, and more on cultivating a healthy lifestyle in general. This mindset fosters patience and sustainability, both of which are important for long term success.

So while we are well aware of some of the reasons why a practitioner may want to become more skilled in providing hypnosis and related service to overweight clients, I'd like to now address some of the reasons why a one may choose *not* to work with a weight loss client. It's important to respond to some limiting beliefs that may be keeping you from being as successful as you can be:

1) You are overweight yourself so you don't feel qualified to help people lose weight. Many practitioners believe (and have been told) that they won't be effective in helping clients achieve healthier bodies if they, themselves, are in need of improvements.

While I agree that it is sometimes preferable to be congruent with the services we offer to the public, I don't agree that we are unable to help people make positive changes unless we have overcome all of our own challenges ourselves. Now, some people just aren't that concerned about being overweight, or being a smoker, or leading a sedentary lifestyle...and other people are concerned with those things and these are the ones who are seeking out our help.

If you are happy with where you are physically, good for you! If you are not, make a plan, find some helpful resources and get to work. Wherever you are on that spectrum, if you are staying away from working with weight loss clients until you are at your perfect goal weight, please consider *not* waiting!

As a woman who has had a varying body size over the years, I will admit that there have been times when I felt dissatisfied and even self-conscious about my weight and I continue to strive for better health in all ways. But, I have also found that many of my weight loss clients tell me that they feel reassured, knowing that I understand a bit about how they feel. And, when I can share personally what helps me, it motivates them even further.

10

There are mixed opinions about whether we should even acknowledge our own personal challenges to a client – some believe that it may hinder our authority and influence while others are convinced that showing our vulnerability can add to the therapeutic process. I'll leave that for you to decide, if this is relevant for you. Or, maybe, you will experiment like I have and find just the right response for you and your clients.

Regardless, there is compelling evidence that the *belief* of the practitioner is paramount in creating success within a client. This is true whether you are a hypnotist, a doctor or a parent! So, if you are struggling with a limiting belief about whether you can be effective in helping people lose weight through hypnosis, that's a good place to start change and I hope what I share within this book will help.

2) You haven't had much success in this area so far so you doubt your ability to help people lose weight. This can happen; unless you've been fortunate enough to receive some good training for helping hypnotically with weight loss, it's easy to get discouraged. If you initially received limited instruction in working with weight loss and have found that your clients aren't making much headway, take a breath.

My best teachers have been my clients and you are about to benefit from the many amazing people who have taught me how to better help them!

3) You simply just don't like, or you are uncomfortable around, overweight and obese people. There, I said it. And it should also be mentioned that if that's the way you feel, then perhaps you are suffering from a limiting perspective because somewhere, somehow, you learned how to feel that way and like any other learned reaction, it can be changed. If you want to change it, that is.

 Besides, fostering what Carl Rogers referred to as *unconditional positive regard* for others is a two-way street; finding the lovable in others helps us see it in ourselves and vice versa.

What Exactly Do You Offer?

While this guide isn't a course on how to market your hypnotherapy practice, I would be remiss if I didn't include some details when it comes to accessing and gaining weight loss clients in particular.

Let's start with how you actually identify your weight loss services for advertising purposes. Perhaps you've heard that advice about not talking about weight "loss" because when a person "loses" weight, why, they'll just try to find it again! This mindset makes sense only in an isolated context, totally disregarding all of the wonderful frames and associations tied to losing weight, like "finding" relief, comfort, energy, self-esteem and more. Believe me, during your several sessions with a client, you will notice that myth easily and automatically being de-bunked.

Additionally, the top search phrase in this genre through web search engines is "hypnosis for weight loss", not "hypnosis for weight release" or some other description. Utilize the language preferred by your potential clients and that will resonate best with their conscious and unconscious awareness.

And, yes, I have had a few clients come in who insisted that they don't want to "find the lost weight again". I simply smile and tell them, "Don't worry. We'll make sure it's gone...permanently...and when you think of it being gone...permanently...what does that look like (or feel like) to you?"

However you offer your services, whether it's through life coaching, hypnosis or another form, be sure that it's clear to a potential client what they will get from you. Many people are confused by the proliferation of programs available and making yours easy to grasp will help distinguish you from the rest of the offerings.

You will probably want to design a program that includes either a series of sessions or you may choose to offer clients a time-defined product, such as a six or twelve month coaching contract. When it comes to achieving sustained change, if we promote the idea that it can take time to safely lose a lot of weight we are also suggesting that a client embrace patience.

Pointing out that most people didn't get to their current weight and health status overnight and it will likely take some time to recover their ideal body is a realistic approach. I would rather not work with clients who expect overnight weight loss results because they also tend to quickly become discouraged and soon abandon our work.

The typical program that I offer consists of a series of six hypnosis sessions. I explain that the first three or so are conducted fairly close together, perhaps a week to ten days apart, with the remaining ones paced out further, according to the individual's needs.

I offer two payment structures for this program. Clients can either pay my regular single session fee, due at the time of each appointment, or they can purchase the program up front and enjoy a discounted price. Many of my clients do purchase the package deal and while that is great for my cash flow it's even more valuable to a client's commitment level.

There's a belief that clients will not value our services if they are discounted or even pro bono. I will dispute that as I have found some of my most motivated clients are the ones who are struggling financially. Perhaps it's the idea that I am the one taking a chance on them that makes them work even more toward improvement. The key to having success with someone who isn't paying much or any money is to be able to use your own judgment and instinct in the selection process.

For example, one of my clients was a young woman in her twenties, a single parent of three children who happened to be an ex-prostitute. She was attending college, pursuing her nursing degree. It was not a difficult decision to take her on as a pro bono client – who wouldn't admire her determination to change her life?! She responded beautifully to hypnosis and it was a joy to be part of her improving life journey.

On the other hand, a woman who offered a story of being widowed and having no money forgot to remove her huge diamond ring. She also parked her fancy new car right in front of my office! When I stuck firm to my fee schedule, she soon agreed and signed up for the program. She experienced success, too, by the way.

Now, not every client will use all of their sessions, for a variety of reasons. The best reason, of course, is that they are having success and decide they don't need any more sessions. Another excuse is the opposite: they are not losing weight and have lost belief in the hypnotic process. Or, they may be distracted or overcome by some crisis or demand in their lives. In any case, communication is vital. If a client doesn't attend a scheduled session, I get in touch and find out what is going on and how I might help get them back on track.

Be clear in the beginning about whether you issue cash refunds. While I have only been asked to refund unused session fees on a couple of occasions, I acquiesced; it's better to have a somewhat satisfied client than one who will negate your reputation.

Note: Do check your local governing regulations as to how you need to manage funds that are paid in advance for services – some require that you safeguard the money in a separate account until the sessions have been completed.

Finding Clients

As mentioned, one of the most frequent ways clients find us is through an online search. It's imperative to have a web presence - preferably your own website and within that site, a section addressing how you help people achieve weight loss goals. Be specific about that, by the way, since weight issues obviously can include being underweight, struggling with eating disorders, etc.

Remember that your website is a public view into not only your hypnosis, coaching or other wellness practice, it's also a glimpse into who you are as a person. This is important because potential weight loss clients are looking to find someone who can help them and that someone needs to be a person with whom they feel a safe connection.

While it is not true of every person who struggles with their weight, a vast majority of them have experienced discrimination, shaming and other negative input. The last place they want to risk more of that is when seeking out and hiring someone like you!

Here are some tips to making your presence within your website appealing, yet professional:

Include a recent photo of yourself. Just like with internet dating, if you present yourself as 20 years younger or 30 pounds lighter, once you meet in person, that other party is going to feel that you are insincere and there goes the trust level, before you have even really started! Use a photo that shows your eyes and a genuine smile. Don't show off your muscles or your cleavage, if you have them – that shouldn't be your primary selling point unless you are trying to attract a type of clientele that will base your work together largely on your physical attributes. So, keep it welcoming, but professional.

Have clean navigation. Use your home page for a brief welcome and description of your service; include a list of specific issues you work with, each of which links to a separate page with details.

Include your fee schedule. Just like with other services, there is a wide range of prices for hypnosis for weight loss. Why not tell your client the cost up front and save both of you the time and trouble, particularly in cases where they can't or won't pay your price? In fact, many potential clients won't bother to call for the rates because they will assume you are too expensive when you don't display your fees on your website.

Some people include an introductory video on their site. I think that's a good idea as it sure shows a curious person who you are and how you speak. It becomes a problem when it's more than just a few minutes long – you will lose the listener when you go on and on, especially if you are talking about yourself!

The person you need to refer to most often on your website is the potential client. Research shows that language containing frequent "you", "yourself" and other references to the potential client is much more enticing than talking about yourself or your business. Make sure that your homepage mentions points that a reader may resonate with because it's here within this first connection that you are forging a working relationship.

Here's one example of how to appeal to a weight loss client:

Patter Box

> *Have you tried just about everything to lose that excess weight? Perhaps this has left you feeling hopeless, thinking that you are stuck for the rest of your life being overweight. Well, you aren't the only one who has felt that way! You may even be surprised to hear that hypnosis* ...(list ways in which hypnosis can help).

Let's talk about testimonials for a bit. While I have a few written testimonials on my website, I never ask clients for them. If a happy client offers me one, I am pleased and may use it to promote my services, but I have an ethical conflict with soliciting testimonials from someone over whom I have hypnotic influence. But, if you are lucky enough to get a client to agree to having their "before" and "after" photos displayed on your website, that's an incredibly compelling influence upon a potential client.

Note: This is also why I don't sell any products in conjunction with my hypnosis services, by the way. I personally don't find it fair or appropriate to take advantage of a client who is welcoming me to help them make a multitude of decisions – it's enough that they have decided to hire me for hypnosis and I don't want to influence their purchase choices unless they specifically request me to.

In addition to having an effective website, people need to be able to find it easily, so you want to use effective SEO (Search Engine Optimization). Consult a web expert if you don't know how to do this yourself.

Getting listed on Google, Yelp, and online hypnosis directories can also help drive potential clients to your website. Understand that signing up for Yelp also opens you up to posted reviews from the public; good or bad – you can be stuck with them. You will also probably get inundated with phone calls from the marketing department at these "free" sites, hoping you will sign up for one of their deals. Remember, there's no such thing as a good free lunch!

I know that some hypnosis practitioners maintain a listing with Psychology Today and get steady client business through it. You can get an initially-free listing and then after a time, pay a monthly fee for inclusion. Keep in mind that often, clients who search with it are looking for mental health therapy and may be confused, thinking that you have psychotherapy training and licensing credentials.

If you have some decent writing skills, a regular blog is another way to reach people. I've had several articles published in online magazines that have resulted in being able to help clients all over the world. It's a good idea to have on hand someone who will proof-read and even edit your writing – you want to insure that it reflects the same quality of the service you are offering.

A few years ago, it was frowned upon to glean customers from your FaceBook readership. People were urged to clearly separate their personal and professional presence in this medium and maintain a business "page" in order to garner as many "likes" as possible. Well, I have ignored all of that and currently have just one account. I use my FaceBook presence to teach people about hypnosis and more importantly, to get to know who I am as a person.

As a result, I do regularly receive private inquiries from my followers about working with me. Since they already feel a sense of familiarity with who I am and what my values are, it's even easier for us to be successful together. Communicating via FaceBook messaging is often very convenient, too, and some of my clients love the feel of instant access for appointment scheduling, sharing files and other resources.

FaceBook private groups afford us an easy way to create and build specialty forums. In 2014, I started my private group for women who work in the field of hypnosis, Hypnotic Women. This group has grown to be an important part of many female practitioners' online experience. I did not start the group with the intention of profiting, other than gaining in friendship and wisdom. But, by sharing my perspectives, along with offering support, I have gained respect as a valued mentor and am often requested to help some of my colleagues resolve their own personal challenges. My relationships online have also allowed me to sell several hypnosis-related books...including the one you are reading!

Even in private forums, managing confidentiality is vital and this can be managed by not revealing identifying aspects such as names, professions, locations and even gender of clients in cases you mention. Some clients are happy to share their success stories and you can ask them to sign a release form allowing you to do so. I've had some weight loss clients who are so proud of their new bodies that they have granted me permission to show the world what hypnosis can do!

Referrals from Clients

One of the best sources of new clientele are referrals from your previous and current clients because there is nothing like a believer to set expectation up front for us. I always provide an appointment card to my active clients, along with a few extras to share.

A question that I might ask a new client is, "Who knows that you are using hypnosis to get healthier?" Sometimes, they will mention specific people or they may say that they are keeping it private, for now. I always agree, whatever the answer is, and suggest, "Won't it be fun to tell them...once you have achieved success?"

Obviously, this is a strategy for future pacing, but it also benefits the hypnosis industry in general. If we are to become an integrated part of healthy lifestyles, we need more of our clients talking about how hypnosis helped them. Encouraging a client to share their experience with others can also inspire others...leading them to using hypnosis for themselves!

Letting people in their life know that they are using hypnosis can create a special level of accountability and support for clients. I recall a particular nursing professional who came to me for virtual gastric band hypnosis. She told her entire team at work what she was going to do and on the day of her "procedure", they gave her flowers and cards. She went home following our session to "recover" from the hypno-surgery. Needless to say, this woman experienced excellent results from our work!

Medical Professionals

Another obvious source of weight loss clients are your local medical professionals, doctors, nurses, and other practitioners who are trying to help people resolve those many weight-related complications.

Regardless of whether my client has any of these problems, I always ask if I can let their doctor know that we are working together. Most clients agree and even welcome my interaction with their doctor. I thank them for allowing me to be part of their healing team.

Following our initial meeting, I send a letter to the client's doctor, letting them know that their patient is using hypnosis to help with weight loss (and any other relevant issues). I include a stamped-self addressed envelope, along with some business cards and rack cards. The letter asks the doctor to sign, note anything I need to be aware of and return it to me. Many doctors do return it to me and several have contacted me for more information. When requested, I will notify the doctor of their patient's progress, but I have found most clients want to surprise their doctors themselves!

Doing this consistently opens the door for relationships with the medical community. Once patients begin to find success through hypnosis, their doctors are delighted – we are making their jobs easier!

I also encourage clients who are feeling better to tell their doctors that they are using hypnosis. Imagine patients who are finally being able to sleep without medication, or healing from surgeries faster, or finding relief from chronic pain, along with losing weight naturally and easily...this definitely will get medical professional's attention!

In fact, don't be surprised if these hard-working folk start lining up for some hypnosis help for themselves. Michael Ellner and I spend the first half of our book, "Hope is Realistic, A Physician's Guide to Helping Patients Take Suffering Out of Pain", addressing how doctors can feel better to heal better.

One of the first doctors to access me for help was trying to deal with chronic migraines. Within a couple of sessions, the migraines started to abate, the doctor became a believer and since then has channeled dozens of clients my way.

Gyms and Health Clubs

One of the best workshops I have experienced was held at a local Curves studio. The owner promoted the free 90-minute presentation I offered and the room was packed. People are just so interested in hypnosis and people who are trying to improve their bodies and their health are even more fascinated.

While the topic of my talk was centered around hypnosis for weight loss, it soon became clear to my audience how important it is to resolve those varied influences that create and maintain the weight problem! As I asked how many in the audience had pain, or sleep, or stress issues, the nodding heads reinforced the point I was making. So, when presenting to a group, don't be afraid to color outside of the weight loss lines!

Service Organizations

Community service clubs are always looking for dynamic and entertaining speakers and if you are adept at talking to groups, you will be in demand. I can get a speaking gig in my county pretty easily...and some will even pay you for your time.

Women's groups in particular are very interested in hearing about how hypnosis can help with weight loss. You can have a lot of fun if your talk is during their breakfast or lunch hour (it often is). I remember one group that was in danger of running past their allotted meeting time simply because the mindful eating strategy I had engaged them in slowed their eating down significantly.

Chapter Two First Contact

Your first live contact with a potential weight loss client is crucial: you may only have a few minutes to help a person gain confidence in what you have to offer, so you had better make it good! Let's talk about the different ways an inquiry may present itself:

1. In person. You're at a social or business gathering and get the opportunity to speak about what you do. You'll find that most everyone is curious about whether hypnosis can help them with a specific need. You'll also learn of any previous hypnosis experience they have had, whether it was watching a stage show, having a private session or hearing about someone else's encounter.

2. An email. Lots of folk feel more safe emailing us, as if they believe that will give them a buffer over our perceived hypnotic powers! I make a point of responding as soon as possible, giving a succinct answer to their inquiry without saying too much. Why? I want to speak with a potential client in person, at least via telephone, so that I can better gauge whether hypnosis and myself are a good fit for them and vice versa.

3. A phone call. People who telephone are often more ready to commit to change. After all, it takes some nerve to pick up the phone and call a strange hypnotist! I have only a few minutes to not only sell them on hypnosis but on my services in particular. Funny, once I stopped trying so hard to sell, clients started buying much more often. Just be yourself and listen. Here are a few points that will help you close the deal when it comes to getting weight loss clients:

- Limit your conversation to 10 minutes or so.
- Ask them questions – you are interviewing them as a potential client. I want to have a high success rate so I screen clients for readiness.
- Provide a brief explanation of how you work.
- Explain your program fee and payment options.

- Tell them about the IRS Tax Credit allowed for weight loss hypnosis. (For USA practitioners.)
- Suggest they check for possible insurance/HSA coverage.
- Offer two potential appointment times.
- Offer a free consultation at your discretion.

4. A phone message. Most of us independent hypnosis practitioners answer our own phone. That means that whether you are working with a client or out kayaking, your answering service picks up the call. Some people hire a live-person service and that can help, but it also means that person had better know a bit about hypnosis and about you! I have found it works just fine to call potential clients back, as long as I can do that within a day or so.

If I reach their answering message, I am careful to just say my name and that I am returning their call, along with a good time to reach me. Treat initial contact with utmost privacy in mind.

5. A text. I don't usually receive an initial inquiry via text but it can still happen. If I do, I often refer them to my website to verify that they have read about me and my services. I also ask if there is a good time to speak on the phone about how I can help. I'm cool with texts from clients once we've started out work – it's often easier and more convenient than phone messaging. I do not answer texts after regular business hours or on weekends, though, and this helps maintain professional boundaries.

6. An inquiry from a friend or relative of a client. This is a tricky one. Sometimes, I'll get a message from someone who knows someone I've helped. While it's great that a previous client is creating belief that hypnosis works, there is no guarantee that it will be as successful with their friend or relative! I treat these contacts pretty much the same as I would any unrelated one but take advantage of any positive influence from that former client.

I take care not to reveal anything to either party about my work with either of them, including the fact that I have started to work with a referred client. I leave that up to my clients to discuss, if they wish.

7. When someone calls about hypnosis for someone else. Unless it's a parent asking about how I might help their minor child, I encourage the caller to have the potential client contact me directly. Not only can we get in a tight spot with confidentiality issues, we really need the client to be motivated on their own for best results.

About Guarantees

You need to make your own decision about whether you will guarantee your hypnosis service. What does that mean, anyway? Will you guarantee it will work? Do what degree? For how long? I often smile when I see the words "Lifetime Guarantee" written on some product because I well know how quickly businesses come and go.

Some practitioners do offer a guarantee of sorts, promising that a client can return for no-cost "tune-ups" anytime that they need. That's nice. I want my clients to feel welcome to come back and get any further help they need but I also value my time and charge them for it. If a potential client asks if I provide a guarantee, my stock answer is, "I guarantee I will do my best to help you succeed." They are satisfied with that.

Patter Box

> *Sounds like you have suffered enough, are you ready to feel better?*
>
> *I'm so glad that you called me because I can help you!*
>
> *It must feel good to be taking action, because you've been thinking about this for a while, haven't you?*
>
> *Would you like to come meet with me for a free consult or do you prefer to get right to work?*

Making a Safe Space

You've probably learned some ways to quickly create a connection with a client that fosters rapport and creates influence, such as pacing and leading, mirroring and matching, etc. I'm going to leave all of that to the NLP experts and instead talk to you about what I believe is the most important thing to do when working with your client: active listening.

Active listening starts within yourself by taking the time to become centered, clearing away distractions and even preconceptions about the experience yet to come. Sure, we can study up and consider specific approaches and tools we may want to utilize for a certain presenting issue but, really, it's best to wait until you are face to face with a client and then trust your instinct when it comes to taking action.

First, you need to make that space for your own mind to settle and become the best it can be for your work together. I use any one of a number of clearing, calming protocols, from an anchor collapse like the Emotional Detox Technique described in the next chapter, to a breathing exercise or maybe a short walk outdoors. My goal is to release distractions and allow not only my mind, but my body, to feel balanced and confident.

Surprisingly, this can be done fairly quickly, especially if you have been practicing it for a while. Nowadays, it takes less than a minute for me to move into a great space for helping clients. If you are new at this, consider practicing this type of state shifting and it will become more automatic for you.

Next, you will want to set an intention of being present with your client. One of the deterrents to great communication occurs when we are caught up thinking about what we are going to do for lunch, or what tool we will next use, instead of really paying attention to what someone else is telling us. And, if you are trying to use some rapport-building strategies, this can also backfire if they feel unnatural or forced.

Here are some tips on how you can stop being in your own head and really be with your client:

1. Engage in mindfulness. Forget the clock for a while. Really take in what is being said, along with what is not being said.

2. Feel the energy that is present. Is there something that you can do to enhance a natural flow between you and your client? Shifting body position or otherwise using body language may be required.

3. Acknowledge and repeat back what you understand. This will not only make your client feel as if they are being listened to, but heard. And, it will ensure that miscommunications do not prevail – super important when it comes to creating and applying change work strategies. Simple misunderstandings applied during the suggestion stage later can blow everything apart!

4. Listen more and talk less, while being as devoid of judgment as possible. If you feel a niggling personal response to something your client is revealing, acknowledge it and set it aside for later, when you have the time and privacy to deal with it. Of course, the counter warning for this is if your danger radar is activated – listen to it and respond in a timely manner.

5. Be open to hearing just about anything. In my earlier years of practice, I was often a bit shocked at how quickly clients would reveal graphic details to me but I learned how to just breathe my way through it without showing concern. And when a client suddenly bursts into tears within minutes of sitting down, I simply hand them a tissue and tell them that I buy boxes of them by the gross and isn't it great that they feel safe enough to let go?!

This goes for other physical responses, too. Realize that clients can twitch, itch, sneeze, cough, fart and even have spontaneous erections. Roll with it, if possible.

Time Management

Once you get going, do keep track of time. In another life, I worked as a driving instructor and am I glad for that experience! After all, riding in a car with brand new drivers and some very old ones made me pretty resilient and it now takes a lot to rattle me. Another valuable thing I gained from that career is an accurate perception of time passing – a typical driving lesson consisted of 60 minutes and I had to become adept at taking a student onto the road, getting through the required tasks and back to the driving school on time.

I use this same skill when working with a hypnosis client. I know pretty much what my goal is for the hour we are spending together and I make sure that we stay on track so that we can get back to the office on time!

Now, one of the ways that it's easy to get detoured when working with a weight loss client is by getting high-jacked by their story. We make a conscious effort to create a safe place for them to drop their guard and share with us all of their struggles, the difficult challenges they have endured, and this often includes some pretty personal and painful stuff. It can be daunting to have to interrupt them just so that we can stay on a time schedule.

Here's how I handle this: I allow a client a limited amount of time to relay their story. I often guide them, especially if they start going down some less-relevant tangent, by bringing them back to why they are here with me. I might say, "And I hear how that may have installed the (perceived influence) that lead to your current weight problem ...thank you for explaining that." This tactic automatically brings the client back to the present and I can now better move them along in our work.

If the client continues to veer back in that direction, I might even clarify to them that, "Since I am not a talk therapist, you don't even have to share all of that with me – it's none of my business!" I have said this early on when a client is overly talkative and time is slipping by. Delivery is everything, though, so stay open and friendly even as you are detouring the conversation. Humor is a great pattern interrupt, as is dropping your notebook on the floor or snapping your fingers and saying, "I just remembered…we only have so much time today and I want you to get the best use of it!"

It's not important that we know all of the details of a person's life experiences. It **is** important that we pick up on how they perceive and otherwise feel about their life and we can get the gist of that fairly quickly. When we filter through this, it becomes even easier for our client to take a similar perspective and be able to notice the themes and the trends that relate to their problem. This kind of awareness allows for them to begin to get a handle on things.

I promote this awareness by asking simple questions, such as, "What behaviors seem to lead to your weight problem?" Once a client identifies some of the behaviors, I will ask, "And when you are doing that, how are you feeling?" or, "And right before you do that, how are you feeling?"

I want to determine how much, if any, a role the emotions are playing. Some clients may insist that they aren't an emotional eater at all and it's true that's not a major problem for everyone. I do ask every client to pay attention during the time between our first and second appointments in particular to their emotional settings whenever they are craving or indulging in unhealthy eating patterns.

This accomplishes two things: the client gains awareness of emotional triggers and I gain further information about what may need to be addressed in that area, along with fodder for the upcoming suggestive work in hypnosis. You can have a written survey for your clients that asks these types of questions, but I personally prefer to discover them in conversational form as that helps the client and I get to know each other better in the process. Either way works, as long as you get those details out in the open so that you can come up with solutions.

Wheel of Life Assessment

In order to be permanently successful with weight loss, awareness of what is working and what is not working in their life is required. Here's a fun and revealing way to help a client discover how balanced their life really is and to create a clear objective for your work together.

On a paper or white board, draw a large circle. Partition the circle into eight sections. Ask your client to designate each segment as an area of their life that is important to them. Some of their answers might include:

Physical Health   Family   Spouse   Home   Friends   Work
Leisure Activities/Fun   Spirituality/Religion   Creativity

Once they have selected their aspects of life, suggest that if the center of the circle represents zero satisfaction and the outer edges represents 100% satisfaction, have them indicate with a line how they rate each of these aspects. When they are finished, they will have an image that looks somewhat like this:

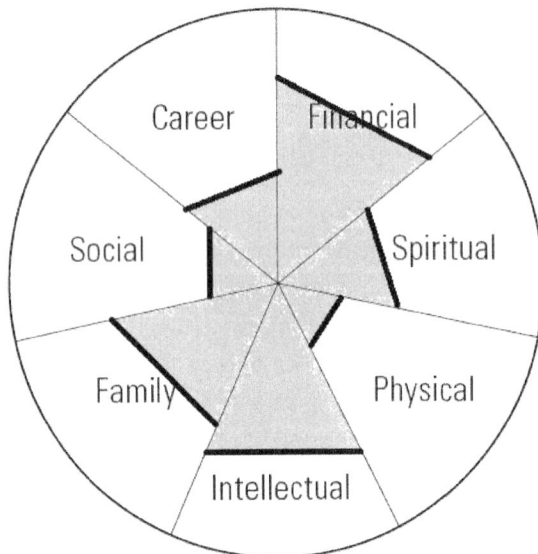

You can have them color in the shaded parts, if you have time, discussing what they are noticing. But the main point, as you can see, is made when you ask them, "If this were the Wheel of Your Life, driving down the road, how smoothly do you think it's rolling?"

A wheel that specifically addresses a client's weight/health goals will be even more detailed. Imagine how it would look, with sections for eating choices, hydration, support resources, physical activity, and more.

You can then help your client create a map for getting things into balance and decide what areas hypnosis will be able to positively influence.

Tip: Do this assessment yourself first to discover your own state of balance.

Identify Influences

Anyone who works extensively with weight loss knows that it's not really about the food; eating just happens to be the distraction that many use in an attempt to avoid or otherwise deal with whatever the real problem is. So, it's not uncommon for a client to come to us wanting to lose weight and it eventually becomes clear there is something deeper and even more important to address.

Some of the typical contributors to weight gain and retention include:

- Excess Stress/Anxiety
- Pain/Discomfort
- Sleep Issues
- Abuse/Guilt/Shame
- Grief/Loss
- Aging/Slowing Metabolism
- Sedentary Lifestyle

Identify, Clarify and Prioritize Goals

One of the challenges we run into when helping a client define their weight loss goals, and how they will know when they have reached them, is knowing what *is* a healthy goal. I make sure that I ask my client what they think is realistic and healthy for them at their current age and lifestyle.

It's counter-productive and potentially even dangerous to encourage a 75 year old with brittle bones and arthritic knees to believe that he will regain all of the strength and vigor of the body from his youth. Mostly, setting unrealistic goals sets a person up for failure when they realize that they are impossible to achieve.

That being said, most people are capable of much more than they can ever imagine and I find that a large percentage of my clients are underachievers when it comes to self-care. I apply my own realistic enthusiasm and belief in their ability to change when it comes to goal setting.

Some clients set their goals in body weight measurement while others prefer to use clothing size or even the idea of remembered or hoped-for abilities, such as being able to walk longer distances or get down on the floor to play with a child. I love it when I get these kinds of details that tell me a person is really imagining and feeling what it will be like to achieve their weight loss goal.

In fact, when a client mentions something like, "I'll be able to slip into that little black dress that's hanging in the back of my closet..." I make a note of that and then, nearly immediately, I begin to utilize that reference. There's a reason her (or, his!) imagination served up that tidbit and I intend to get all of the fuel I can from it.

For clients who show a trepidation or dislike for the weighing scale, I take some time to reframe that, clarifying to them that it's kind of pointless to have an emotional response to an inanimate object that doesn't have any feelings in return...and wouldn't it be more useful to think about the scale as the tool it is? It's a valuable instrument that will be showing, right there, in black and white, the concrete and empowering change...measuring in mere ounces the improvement, the health gains...even as it reveals the weight loss!

Sometimes, it's as simple as asking a client whether they plan on weighing themselves once a week...or twice a week. It's a fact that people who are successful at losing weight and maintaining a healthy weight consistently use their scale as a valuable ally.

As you can see, I grab every opportunity in seemingly casual conversation to use a flow of language to direct, detour and otherwise guide a client in a helpful direction. It's easy, once you know the value of doing so and when you do it organically, the client remains comfortable and simply floats along your desired course.

Chapter Three   Hope into Belief

Even before you conduct a formal client intake, you are gathering fodder for your work with the client. From the moment you initially interact, each of you are assessing, judging and otherwise measuring how you will fit and how effective the therapeutic relationship will be. A vital part of your job is to expand **hope**, which is what led the client to you, into **belief** and you need to accomplish this as soon as possible. We know the power of expectation when it comes to making positive changes and we also want to instill that from the beginning.

There are several ways to establish belief, or as they say in the movie industry, to suspend disbelief in a client, so that they are able to move past doubt, skepticism and fear. During the pre-talk, I explain to a client that we can find belief in the possibility of change from different places:

1) We might look to the past, in which case we would find examples of successful change in a person's life, whether that has to do with weight loss or other topics, even relatively small victories.

2) We might also look to the future, or even to an alternate universe, creating a template for their mind-body to follow. Here is where I introduce the idea that our inner mind is the Great Eavesdropper, using our thoughts about our future as building blocks to get there. When we utilize hypnosis to do that, the subconscious grabs onto it as a blueprint, automatically moving in that direction.

Accordingly, when a person makes the mistake of worrying about what they are afraid might happen, the subconscious takes that as a command. This happens because the aspects of judgment and discernment over whether this is a helpful direction or not are not managed in that realm – these are conscious thought processes, for the most part.

This perspective helps a client begin to understand the value of inputting positive and motivating thoughts, emotions and imagery into their mind. I often tell this story to further relay how it works:

Two Wolves

This story is attributed to the Cherokee Nation, but I don't know the actual author. Oral tradition is used by Native American culture to pass on wisdom, and I think this one is wonderful.

The grandfather of the tribe was speaking to the children one day and he said, "Inside each of us are two wolves, battling for control. One wolf thrives on hatred, anger, resentment, pain, and jealousy. The other wolf thrives on kindness, forgiveness, generosity, compassion and love."

One of the children asks, *"Grandfather, which wolf wins?"*

The grandfather replies, *"The one you feed."*

When we help a client begin to feed their "good wolf", things start to get better!

Tip: It's easy to take stories like the one above and frame it for weight loss. Here's how I did it in a meme I shared on FaceBook:

There is a battle between forces going on inside of you...one part of you that doesn't care about your health, your feelings or your real desires and another part of you that desperately wants you to thrive and live a long and happy life. Which of these forces will win?
The one you feed.

3) Finally, we can help establish belief early on in our work when we give a person the experience of the power of their own mind. A perfect venue for this is to teach the client how to quickly and easily shift states.

Note: Most weight loss clients are distressed on some level about something; even people who say they live a relatively stress-free life but are overweight are experiencing the stress of being overweight.

Patter Box

> *Repetition is key for making changes. That's how those unhelpful eating habits got hard-wired into your brain. We're going to rewire things so that you change your thoughts and behavior and lose the weight...so it will take not only a few sessions with me, but you will be doing some things on your own to help with that, including listening to some hypnosis recordings I will provide.*

To quickly build belief in the client's ability to use their own mind for change, I often use the Emotional Detox Technique from my HOPE Coaching program, designed with Michael Ellner and Alan Barsky. I will introduce it as an easy-to-do and quick remedy for moving out of unhelpful states that may be contributing to unhealthy eating responses.

I'll talk a bit about the brain, and all of the billions of neurons (brain cells) and the way they communicate, creating pathways and neural nets for all sorts of thoughts, reactions and actions. I like the metaphor of making a trail through the woods – the first time you walk it you are blazing a trail. The second, third, tenth, hundredth time you go down it, that path becomes more and more delineated...until it starts to become a rut...or a ditch...or a trench.

This is how habits are created, whether they are desirable or not. I explain that there is a technique that will quickly divert, or detour, the brain and the nervous system itself away from those entrenched pathways. Then I guide a client through it, first telling them they don't need to worry about memorizing the steps because I'll give them a little cheat sheet for it later. I include this in the Appendix at the back of this book. My typical process goes like this:

Kelley: *Before we do any formal hypnosis, I'd like to show you how easy it is for you to get some control over how you are feeling...so that you can practice and feel better between our sessions. I know that when you feel better...you will take better care of yourself. Would you like to play?*

Client: *Okay.*

Kelley: *Great! Now, all you have to do is sit there and place your hands loosely on your legs. This little trick that I am about to show you is super easy to do and it works really fast. You don't have to worry about trying to memorize the steps, because I have them on paper and I'll give them to you. Just follow along and enjoy the process. Ready?*

Kelley: *Good. Now, in the privacy of your mind, just turn your thoughts to something that bugs you. I don't want you to pick anything really major* (like a recent death or other trauma) *but just something that creates a negative feeling...like frustration or worry...maybe how a situation or person makes you feel crappy...Or even, a discomfort or pain that you struggle with. Let me know when you've got it.*

Client nods.

Kelley: *Okay, now notice where in your body you feel that...Because your body is always responding to whatever you are thinking or feeling, whether you are aware of it or not. Where are you feeling that?*

Client describes sensations.

Kelley: *Cool, that's how your body is communicating back to your mind – it's actually working perfectly well, that mind-body dialogue! Now, will you please measure that response – if Zero is none and Ten is super strong, where are you on that scale?*

Client: *About a Five, I guess.*

Kelley: *Good, and you could even make that go higher, couldn't you? That's how powerful your imagination is!*

Client nods.

Kelley: *So, as you are feeling that, at that Five or maybe even more, please make a fist with your left hand.* (taps client's left hand) *Just hold that for a few seconds, imagining all of that emotion, all of that feeling just flowing right into that hand, there. Good. Now open your hand and take a nice, deep, cleansing breath...and exhale. Gently close your eyes...and open them.*

Now, will you please imagine, in whatever way works for you, imagine...that you are having a wonderful day...you are doing something you really enjoy...perhaps you are there by yourself, maybe you are there with someone you love. You notice how good you feel...you have a smile on your face...it's a perfect hair day! Your heart is happy, your mind is peaceful...your spirit is playful...Got it? Good...

Now, with your other hand, (taps on hand) *your left hand, make a fist...let's anchor all of these wonderful feelings in this hand, here. Hold it...hold it...and open your hand.*

Take another deep, cleansing breath...close your eyes...Let your thoughts drift a bit...I like to think of my thoughts as being leaves...leaves falling gently from a tree...into a stream of moving water...going to wherever thoughts go when we don't need them anymore...That's right...

39

Now, open your eyes and here is where the magic happens: please place both hands into fists...and we count down... 5...4...3...2...1...Open your hands, one more cleansing breath in...and out. Good!

How do you feel now? Pretty good?

Client nods and smiles.

Kelley: *Awesome...and, when you go back to find that original, disturbing thought or feeling, where did it go?!*

Client: *Wha??*

Kelley: *Isn't that crazy? You were experiencing that at about a Five or more, where is it now?*

Client: *Maybe a One or so...wow!*

TIP: If the client didn't experience a noticeable shift, repeat the technique.

Kelley: *And it will work, every time you use it. In fact, the more often you use it, the more effective it will be...and eventually, you'll find that you automatically spend more time over here* (tapping on the positive anchor hand)*...and won't that make life better?*

Client agrees.

Kelley: *And what I really like about this is that YOU get to choose how you'd rather be feeling. I gave you some suggestions for this state* (tapping on client's left hand again) *but you filled it in really well on your own. Can you imagine a time when perhaps you are coming home from work, and you are stressed and tired...but your* (family member) *is waiting to spend some time with you? You could use this technique to bring in feelings that would relax or maybe even energize you?*

Or, maybe you want to study and learn something, but you can't seem to settle down and focus because your mind is being distracted by some worry. Imagine putting the worry in that hand, there and then using this hand, here, to shift into a great learning state!

When do you think you might use this technique?

Client: *Well, maybe before I eat?*

Kelley: *Yes! That's brilliant! It would probably help you eat more mindfully, right? When would be another time to make yourself feel better?*

Client: *Before sleep. Maybe if I have an argument with someone...*

Kelley: *Perfect, you have got the idea. You can use this tool for a lot of situations and even thought we call it an Emotional Detox, you can use it for pretty much any unwanted thought or feeling...like a food craving, for example. Imagine getting stuck thinking about some food choice that isn't conducive to weight loss...you can move out of that very easily and quickly, into a place where you feel strong and motivated.*

Or, if you have some pain going on...you can quickly reduce the suffering of that pain. I've taught this to many clients who have chronic pain and they find that using it periodically throughout their day helps them tremendously. Sometimes, they are even able to rewire stuck neural pathways that have been mistakenly sending pain signals, even after their body has healed!

Remember when I told you that part of the way hypnosis works is through repetition? That we want to rewire some of the neural pathways in your mind that have been contributing to your weight challenge? Well, this tool will help you do that.

41

In fact, it works really well as a way to stay ahead of unhelpful stress and tension. If you apply it several times a day, it's almost like re-booting your mind, which also helps your physical state. It will help you rise above any challenges during your day, even as your brain is being re-structured. So have fun with it and notice the difference!

Using the Emotional Detox or any other open-eye, conversational technique in the beginning of your work with a client will create belief not only in hypnosis as a powerful change instrument but in the client's ability to make change within themselves. This is gold!

If the client doesn't feel much of a shift, simply repeat the process, mentioning that magic word, repetition, again. Not only will this further change those pathways, it will help the person get more comfortable with generating the change on their own, which is our ultimate goal.

On the very rare occasion when a client doesn't find any relief, just move on. This has happened a few times in my career, usually with clients who aren't following my directions well or are so entrenched in their negative states that they have difficulty finding a more positive one. In these cases, I wait until using more formal hypnotic techniques to access something better – I can always come back and utilize what they found and teach the process again.

Or, I'll just kick that one to the curb. Most often, we offer several approaches until just the right one resonates - the key is to reject the idea of failure and most importantly, avoid making a client feel like they are failing or being resistant. It's not a test!

And, of course, you've probably heard the axiom, "Go there first." This is a reference to the value of experiencing and actively utilizing hypnotic processes ourselves, so that we have firsthand knowledge of what that feels like. The benefits of incorporating the anchor collapse described above into our daily life and hypnosis practice are limitless.

You can use our Emotional Detox Technique to:

- Clear your mind before and after client sessions
- Address your own health and wellness needs
- Reduce overall mental stress and clutter

Step Back to Go Forward

Let's take a step back to move forward...and address finding belief in what we are going to accomplish by going back in time.

One of my guidelines is to utilize age regression approaches primarily in order help people get in touch with positive resource states, thereby reducing potential negative effects such as re-traumatization. This can be as easy as asking a client to think of a time when they accomplished something meaningful – perhaps it had to do with weight or other health improvements but it doesn't necessarily have to.

Some people believe that they have been overweight all of their lives, even though they smile and agree with me when I ask if they have ever looked at a photo of their younger selves and noticed that they actually looked pretty good!

One wonderful fellow that I helped came to me as a last resort. In his 70's and being slowly overtaken by his weight, he felt his whole life was being cut short. When I found out that he had a military background, I asked if he had a photo of himself in those earlier days, when he was fit and healthy.

With a great sense of pride and joy, he happily shared an image of himself, on the beach. He looked like a movie star from a 1950's film! In our first session, he got back in touch with that vibrant young man who turned out to be the Inner Coach he was needing. This client went on to drop nearly 200 pounds of excess weight and got his active and happy life back.

But unless a client has a conscious memory of having been relatively fit, I suggest they focus on some achievement other than weight loss, like an educational or career success, or something else that really made them feel competent and confident and then we anchor that state.

To do this, I ask where they feel that confidence in the body, or perhaps we will objectify it with a sensation, a color or a word. We will increase its intensity, even letting it expand and flow throughout their mind and body. Once they are feeling it at its most powerful, I provide suggestions that whenever they need to recall it, they can become aware of it with their breath, the sensation, the color, the word, etc.

I make sure to refer back to this anchor repeatedly during the rest of the session, in future sessions and even in custom recordings, thereby strengthening the neural net which is managing those feelings of confidence and success.

Visiting the past also provides a powerful opportunity to change perspective, which can make a huge influence on how people are responding currently to life's stimuli. By allowing someone to view their past experiences through a more mature eye we empower them to grow up a part of themselves.

For example, when it comes to changing "kiddie-food" (as my friend, John Cerbone, describes it) preferences, imagine the possibilities! I describe my Inner Child work later in this book.

Patter Box

> *Some clients lose a lot of weight, some lose several pounds...but all of my clients feel better and we know that people who feel better, heal better and take better care of themselves!*

About Scripts

I love reading other hypnotists' scripts. I also love reading stories, poems and even fortune cookie notes. I once created an awesome hypnotic journey for a man that was inspired from the back of a cereal box. And one of my favorite hypnosis audio recordings is a simple rendition of The Beatles', "Lucy in the Sky with Diamonds", by Richard Nongard.

Think of using scripts not only as training wheels while you are learning how to think and speak hypnotically, but also as marvelous sources of continuing learning. The trick to being able to use a pre-written script well lies in:

- Being flexible for your client's needs
- Not sounding like you are reading it (unless, of course, you tell your client that you are)
- Being able to eventually put the script away as you incorporate the ideas and patter into your memory bank

If hypnosis is dependent on the creative imagination, then once you are somewhat comfortable with the actual hypnotizing stuff, you will want to put the script down and trust your own mind to provide what is needed.

I practice stimulating my creativity every day, when I am not with clients. One of the best places for this is when I am driving, believe it or not. I'll pick a topic for the commute and begin to talk to myself out loud and by the time I reach my destination, I'll have some crazy loops that always contain something worth using in my work.

You can also do this while writing. As you may notice, I love to write but I usually do it on my computer. I recently noticed that my keyboard resembles my karate sensei's black belt, which is completely white now due to years of use, and the letters are all worn away from the keys. It's interesting that my fingers can find the letters without me having to think about it. One of my favorite activities is to close my eyes and let my fingers do the hypnotic writing – perhaps you've experienced getting into the flow this way. Even ten or fifteen minutes of this usually creates some interesting piece.

Or, you might like to sit in nature, in the middle of a field or on a mountain top and let all of that glory ignite your creative spark. Forest bathing always gives me spontaneous metaphors from nature that I use later in my work.

So, as I share scripts in this book, please use the bits that resonate not only with you but with your potential clients, but also do your best to improve them and even be inspired to come up with your own. I want you to tickle your creative imagination to become the very creative, fantastic hypnotist that you can be!

Mirror Progression Technique

This process can be used to help create belief in a client for future healing, weight loss and other transformational outcomes. It is crucial for the client to be able to imagine and also hypnotically experience positive change; doing so creates that vital blueprint for the subconscious mind while inciting belief that change is possible.

This mirror technique is one that I typically use in a first session with a client, shortly after providing an induction and then anchoring a safe, relaxing state, suggesting that their body is going to rest and relax there.

Patter Box

> *"And while your body is here, resting and relaxing, let's take that amazing mind of yours and go a little further..."*

This is an interactive process and you may find it helpful to establish some form of communication, such as finger signals or head nod, although this is not always necessary. I refer to a female client in this script, so adjust it accordingly for your client.

Guide the client to view her body in a full length, floating mirror:

See yourself here in this mirror. You may notice that you are wearing the clothing that you wore here to my office today or you may be wearing something else...or, you may not be wearing anything at all. Just notice that you can see yourself, and, that you can see yourself from all perspectives: from the front, from the back, from the sides...from above and below. Let me know when that image is visible to you.

If the client has difficulty visualizing, you can guide their attention to their feet and illuminate them with some light source such as a flashlight. You can also inform them that some people "see" in hypnosis, while others "feel" or just have a sense of things; that however they are aware of that image is just fine.

I want you to not only notice how you look in that mirror, there...but how you feel as you look at yourself in the mirror. Because you have a desire to make some healthy changes by releasing unwanted weight, chances are that you have mixed feelings when you view yourself. I invite you to let those feelings appear; let them drift up. Perhaps some of them are positive, some of them may be neutral and some of them are negative. Let yourself be aware of how you feel as you view yourself in that mirror. (Pause)

Now, I want to tell you that this is a very special mirror...in fact, it's a type of magical mirror. In a few moments, I am going to begin to say some numbers and these numbers will reflect weight release for you. Please continue to look at the image and allow yourself to experience the changes visually, but also to allow yourself to feel the changes occur in your body. Are you ready? Let's begin...

From this point, you can either start by saying a number 5 or 10 lbs. lighter than the client's current weight or you can start by saying the initial weight loss in pounds: i.e., 2 or 5. Some clients prefer to measure their body by clothing size and you can work with that.

Have the client notice how it feels to have that initial weight release, giving suggestions based on their individual case. Proceed in increments toward the desired weight/clothing size.

Tip: Incorporating desired new habits during the various stages will enhance the effectiveness of this experience.

At each step, allow time for the client to notice the shifts. You can suggest that they happen spontaneously, or that they may occur gradually. Let the client know that that image of themselves is not static; it is able to move – this is where you can mention that perhaps she is finding it easier to walk, climb stairs or get out of bed in the morning, etc.

You can suggest that the image is taking on some of the new, healthier behaviors that are allowing this weight release to happen and then insert your client's specific preferences, abilities and needs. Using personal details helps the experience become even more real to your client. The more you can customize this process, the better the response will be as your words begin to merge with their thoughts, becoming powerful suggestions that become effortlessly embedded.

Watch your client as they experience the improvement – often they will smile, laugh or tears will fall as they get in touch with success, increased comfort, confidence and belief that they can achieve their desired goals.

I have watched some clients begin to move their body in response to what they are experiencing – one man slowly begin to sit up straighter, his posture improving, his chin rising...as he took on the traits of his confident, healthy and proud countenance of his improved, lighter future self.

As the hypnotic weight loss progresses, you can incorporate patter such as the following:

Patter Box

> *"If there is something that your weight was preventing yourself from engaging in, see yourself being able to step into that activity..."*
>
> *"By now, you notice that your energy levels are much higher...notice how great you feel!"*
>
> *"Perhaps you have something that has been waiting in the closet for you...try it on...or maybe you have to go shopping for some new clothing. Notice how much more fun trying on new clothes is when you are healthier...slimmer...more comfortable..."*
>
> *"Even though your success seems nearly effortless, please notice what you are doing to make this happen* (insert specific behaviors, attitudes, etc.)

Be sure to focus on the emotions and feelings that are changing as the body is changing. Use compelling and descriptive words such as PROUD, FREE, CONFIDENT, ENERGIZED, REJUVENATED, SUCCESSFUL, INSPIRED, EASY, NATURAL, etc.

Note: Rarely, a client may get "stuck" at a certain weight loss level. They may feel resistance in moving lower or they may even emerge from hypnosis. I have found that it is helpful to investigate any associations to stressful or painful times in their life when they were also at that specific weight. In several of these cases, clients later told me that in previous weight loss experiences, this would, in the past, be the exact point to which they were able to reduce, only to be stopped inexplicably and then begin to regain any lost weight.

One client revealed that as she achieved a certain weight, she felt like she was spinning down a deep hole and she emerged from the hypnosis. Discussing it further, she recalled that the last time she weighed that much, she was going through a difficult divorce. Before we continued, I spent some time helping her neutralize that association so that she could move easily through it toward her goal. This was a fantastic opportunity to show her how easy it was for her to instantly change her emotional responses!

In cases like this, it's not always necessary to address whatever surfaces immediately – you can certainly do this at a later time. I might say something like, "Wow. Isn't it great that you now know this? We can deal with it whenever you want to..." This gives the client a choice and may also allow for some further private exploration and processing, which is usually helpful.

You want to allow the client to eventually settle at the right body size/weight by saying, "As you are nearing your ideal weight and size, I will let you decide what is right for you...what is comfortable for you." It is important to help a client find a realistic weight. If your client continues to want to reduce weight in this experience, to what might be considered an unhealthy level, this can serve as a warning regarding her body perception and expectation.

Once the client is satisfied with the image and the sensations that have been obtained, have her connect with that mirror image of her healthy, future self. From this point continue with:

That woman has something to tell you. She wants you to know that she loves you...that you are never alone, that she is always with you. If you want to let her know how you feel about her, please do so. (pause)

She also wants to ask you something...she wants to know if you will do what you need to do in order to allow her to be revealed, to allow her to come out and play. Will you do that? (get agreement)

Wonderful, you can see how happy that makes her! And, in return, she promises to be there for you, every step of the way, every pound of the way. She will be your own, private coach and cheerleader. She will help you make the right choices so that you will release that unwanted weight comfortable and

50

permanently. If, for any reason, you start to get off track, she will get you back on course...perhaps with a firm guiding hand, or an encouraging word or maybe just by reminding you of all of your very own, powerful reasons for making this improvement in your life.

Next, allow your client to take in that image, integrating this healthy, slimmer part as an inner resource. Provide post hypnotic suggestions that whenever they need to, they can imagine that future self and it will strengthen their ability to release the weight. You can also use the mirror and healthy image in future sessions and custom recordings.

Patter Box

> *Imagine your body...the way you want it to be, the way you wish it to be, the way you will it to be, and the way it will be.*
> ~ Nancie M. Barwick

Changes in the Multiverses

There is another way I use time travel to help a client build belief in our work together and that is to move them around within time and space. Not only can we take people into their futures to see how successful they are, we can take them into alternate universes, parallel universes, multiverses of all kinds to manipulate, create and otherwise lay down the pathways for change.

I love that these adventures are **fun** and I especially appreciate how they take advantage of the idea that the subconscious mind doesn't know that they are fantasy. Just like the way that our dreams can seem real, so, too, can our hypnotic journeys, leaving the subconscious mind reeling with whatever we constructed, believing that it not only happened but is continuing to happen, all for our client's benefit.

In using the concept of alternate or parallel universes for transformation, I use a template from Don Gibbon's playbook to help clients access a wonderful place where all of their dreams not only come true, but where they actually exist. (Don and I recently released our book that is all about these hypnotic multiverses, "Virtual Reality Hypnosis: Adventures in the Multiverse".)

We know that weight problems are often symptomatic of entrenched voids within a person's life, whether those voids are a result of trauma or from current lack of the fulfillment of human needs. Getting a client back in touch with feelings of love and security can make dramatic shifts in the way they are responding to life.

Interestingly, in some cases where a client wasn't able to come see me in person, whether that was due to financial or time constraints, I have shared a recording with them. When these clients did come in for an appointment, many announced that they had "automatically" lost weight, simply by listening daily. Once again, we cannot under value the power of tapping into hypnotic healing states!

Here's a peek into how I use a generic parallel universe approach to help a weight loss client, based on a script from Don Gibbons. Following induction and deepening of your choice:

And now, we are reaching down into the vast, untapped potentials that lie within you...and we are releasing ...wonderful feelings of happiness...and joy...and wonder ...and rapture...and ecstasy...and light. And all of these wonderful feelings are flowing out from your innermost depths, sent by your inner healer...filling...and flooding...very muscle and every fiber, and every nerve of your being, with wave after wave of beautiful, indescribable joy, happiness, wonder, ecstasy, rapture, and delight. For the stronger we can make them, the more effective they will be...in changing your life into a thing of wondrous beauty.

And so, they come flowing out...and flowing out...There's no end to how good you can feel, and no end to how strong we can make them ...for if you weren't hypnotized, you couldn't bear a fraction of the joy, and the happiness, and the wonder, and the ecstasy, and the unimaginable delight that is flowing through every muscle and fiber, and cell and nerve of your body, now, in these golden moments. And the more you feel, the more you're able to feel, and the more you feel, the more you want to feel, and the more wonderful, the more rapturous, the experience becomes. And if you weren't hypnotized, you couldn't bear a fraction of the joy, and the happiness, and the wonder, and the ecstasy, and the unimaginable delight that is yours, now, to savor and experience to the fullest. This is your time...

And flowing...into another universe...where there is no time...there is no space...There is only...a boundless ocean of infinite, unbounded, and everlasting love, at the center of this universe, which is in the center of all other universes. And you feel yourself dissolving into the infinite ocean of boundless rapture, ecstasy, and love, and it's as if all of the happiness, and all of the love, and all of the joy, and all of the wonder, and all of the delight that have ever been felt by all the people who ever walked the face of the earth...are yours...to enjoy ...now...in these golden moments of delight, free from time and free from space.

And in this universe...where anything is possible...in fact, probably...find yourself...your real self...that YOU who is healthy, vibrant...pure. Get in touch with the YOU that is glowing with well-being...filled with love...filled with the purest sense of integrity and self-regard that you desire...that you deserve...Understand that this is the state of your natural birth right...to be whole, to be healthy...Soak it up and make it part of you...

Understand now...that it's only the separation from this infinite ocean of rapture, and wonder, and ecstasy, and delight, which is your home beyond the stars...it's only the separation from this ocean...that is the source of all unhappiness, all depression, all anxiety, all despair...all loneliness.

And celebrate...deeply and profoundly...that you have now re-discovered this place of love and good health...and understand that you can return to it, over and over again...over and over again...to restore your mind and your body...to refill your cup of everlasting love...

And so...as the feelings continue to grow, stronger and stronger, they are becoming infinite in their strength...and infinite in their power...beyond the power of words to describe ...infinite, beyond infinity...and eternal, beyond all measure of Eternity.

And you find yourself floating...and dissolving...into a wave of infinite, unbounded ecstasy, beyond the limitations of time ...beyond the limitations of space...beyond the limitations of the Universe, itself...

Within this healing discovery state, it is more than plausible to help a client get in touch with any number of positive resources from any number of places and times. Life stories can be re-scripted in order to better fit current circumstances and goals. Grief can be resolved, power retrieved and targeted toward health improvement, forgiveness and acceptance experienced; the possibilities are endless!

A memorable client of mine decided to, while drifting in her "Sea of Love", let go of all of her earthly burdens (which were many in number and weight) and swim like a blissful mermaid toward her cosmic twin who represented her true and authentic, slimmer self. They embraced and merged...and thereafter, that inner mermaid became the inspirational inner coach for my client as she continued successfully toward her goals.

Chapter Four   Change the Mind: Change the Body

Raising Emotional Intelligence

In conjunction with teaching a client how to gain mastery over their emotional and behavioral responses, I sometimes find it necessary to help them find clarity over how their emotions are actually serving them (and often, damaging them!)

Describing emotions as important signals from our inner self is an acceptable frame for most people; they can grasp the idea that our emotions capture our attention like a signal. I want to be sure that my client can discern which emotions they need to pay attention to, and which ones they can ignore or otherwise re-wire. Here's how I might do that:

> Kelley: *So, it's important that we get clear about the purpose of an emotion and that we can make the distinction about whether we need to listen to it and respond appropriately to it. For example, if I am in the parking lot at Safeway, at midnight...and I'm feeling some anxiety, that's probably a good thing, right? That response is warning me that this may not be the place to be inattentive to my surroundings, or linger. I'll want to get to my car and get out of there, being aware of the space around me.*
>
> *But, if I am relaxing on my deck, watching the sunset...and I'm feeling anxious, well, that's just baloney! That feeling isn't really serving me anything at the time and it would be just fine to get rid of it with that Emotional Detox technique or maybe some other self-hypnosis, right?*

From here I would ask the client to identify some of the emotions that are "causing" them to eat inappropriately and we could discover if they are signals that need a different response or if they are "stuck" signals that we can alleviate.

For example, perhaps a client is feeling bored at night and finds themselves wandering into the kitchen, looking for something. Helping the client identify the feeling, maybe it isn't really boredom, which I've always considered to be a more of a void or a lack of emotion, but is instead a feeling of restlessness. In this case, this would be a signal from the body that it wants to discharge pent up energy and the correct response might be to stretch, take a walk or maybe to relax in a bath. Eating doesn't really help when the body wants to move or unwind and helping a client find an alternative response that is not only appropriate, but helpful, can really make a difference.

Or, a client might find that every time they get frustrated with their job, they end up eating some junk food. By first identifying what emotion is being expressed, we can then find a better response. The signal of frustration is usually telling us that whatever we are doing isn't working and we need to try something else!

Cal Banyon uses a metaphor of the signals in a car that I find useful – describing how, if the oil light goes on, this indicates that the driver needs to check the oil level in the car. If the driver pulls into the closest fuel station and adds more gas to the tank, this does nothing to help the oil level and it can even be problematic, especially if the gas tank is already full...or if the driver is adding some harmful substance to the tank!

Personally, I wish we were all taught this stuff early on in school. Raising Emotional Intelligence within our clients and ourselves is of great value. If you think about some of the "heavier" emotions that you have personally experienced, you can also get clarity on what they were trying to signal and how you might have responded to them, whether that was helpful or not.

And thanks to neuroplasticity, the more we gain mastery over our emotional responses, the more automatic the more positive responses become!

Here are some other emotions that weight loss clients may struggle with, can you determine what those feelings may be trying to tell a person, along with what a helpful response might be?

Feeling Stressed Out

Loneliness

Anger

Grief/Loss

Frustration

Disappointment

Boredom

Depression

Hopelessness

Helplessness

Motivation and Inspiration

Sometimes, what a client really needs is help getting going. So often, they say, "I just feel stuck," or, "I know I should do something but I can't get started." Luckily, we know some tricks to get them moving in more ways than one.

Here is one of the easiest and most inspiring ways to get a client engaging in self-care: Remind your client that what they are now choosing to do is tantamount to giving their loved ones a very spectacular, priceless gift. Many of my weight loss clients are very loving, kind and generous people; that's probably also why they have ended up neglecting themselves. They have been spending a lifetime caring for others, putting others' needs before their own, until they have arrived at their present state of poor health. Why not utilize how much they care for others by pointing out that they will enhance their loved ones' lives when they take care of themselves?!

I share my own gratitude toward my parents who are, at the time of this writing, 87 and 88 years of age and in remarkably good health, mentally and physically. This can be attributed to several factors beyond genetics: mainly healthy lifestyles and positive mindsets. What a gift they have given me for decades, not having to worry or be stressed out over their health. This also inspires me to take care of my own well-being, so that my children can enjoy the same freedom from stress and worry about their mom!

Additionally, simply reminding a client of all of their very own, very good reasons why they sought you out in the first place can do the trick, especially if we do that in an entranced state of mind. To accomplish this, I use my own version of the good ol' "Fork in the Road" approach – I think you'll like it:

Future Choices

> *Now, imagine that you are standing on the top of a beautiful mountain. You look out over the vista – it's a clear, comfortable day and you feel fine. Take in a couple of wonderful breaths of that fresh, mountain air...and begin to become aware...to sense, in whatever way works for you...that emanating from the very place you are standing...are two golden, translucent lines...one moves off in one direction and the other...in another direction...*

> *You somehow realize that these two lines represent alternate futures...possible futures for you...that are, of course, determined by the choices you make from this point on. It might be very interesting and even inspiring to you if we were to explore these potential futures...to let you get a glimpse, a feel, for what can lie ahead.*

> *So, in a moment, I'll just begin to count, from one to three...and*

as I do, I'd like you to move into that future over there, that one in which you just continue with your same unhealthy behaviors (specify some of them)...Let's go forward in time and see what happens...I'll count and you will move into that future...I don't know how far you will go, maybe you'll go to a year from now, maybe it will be less...maybe it will be more...but when I reach three, there you will be...in that future in which you have continued with these negative and unhealthy habits.

Here we go, one...two...three...arriving there now. Begin to become aware...however it appears to you...of the results of having made that choice to continue to carry with you the burden of all that excess weight...days, weeks, months...perhaps years...of engaging with the unhealthy attitudes and behaviors...that made you gain the weight and keep you overweight.

Notice how you feel...the discomfort...Are you pleased with yourself? Are you happy that you continued along that unhealthy path of eating for reasons other than nurturing your body?

Do you see the remnants of that lifestyle? (Mention specific food preferences/behaviors that contribute to the weight issue.) *Has it been worth it?*

Notice what you have gained...or lost...as a result of having decided to continue to live in this way...Let your subconscious memorize all of this so that it can be utilized to help you.

And, when you are ready, let yourself move back as I count back...from three to one...back to that viewpoint on the mountain top...back to the present time...three...two...one.

And immediately, you feel a great sense of relief. Take in a big breath of that beautiful mountain air and tell yourself how happy you are that that future hasn't happened...and doesn't

59

have to happen...As you turn your focus to the other future...the one that is beckoning now...and as I count, from one to three, you will move forward in time...to a time in the future where all of your weight loss goals have been achieved...I don't know if that will be this year...or in the year to come...but when you arrive, let yourself revel in the joy, the happiness of having achieved this goal.

Ready? Here we go...one...moving forward in time...two...feeling even better...and three, there now...in a time and place where you are feeling so good, comfortable, healthy...Notice everything about it – the sensations of your energized, slimmer body.

The way your clothing fits...how it feels to move your healthy and strong body. Perhaps you have a big smile on your face because it just feels so wonderful to be you!

Maybe you see yourself from afar...or maybe you are looking out of your own eyes...whichever it is, pay close attention to all of the positive benefits of having allowed these changes to happen.

Notice everything about your wonderful, enriched, healthy life and, in particular, notice how happy you are about that decision that you made...back then...to create the changes that brought you to this point.

Let your subconscious now memorize all of these marvelous thoughts, feelings and sensations...imprinting them deeply to make this dream a reality for you.

(Long Pause)

And when you are ready, drift back with my voice, as I count from three to one...back to the present time...three, two...one...

Values

Everyone can identify an idea or belief that they hold close to their heart, a value that is a constant in their life. When we help a client not only identify a value that is amenable with weight loss, such as good health, confidence, living with vitality, etc., but embrace it, some good stuff starts to happen. When one is congruent in choosing a valued direction, unwanted and distracting behaviours are automatically decreased.

Here is a nifty process from Richard Nongard and I have used it with clients of many ages:

> As you relax, imagine you have just received a present. Imagine that this present is a surprise; you don't even know who sent it, but now you are holding it. It won't be a simple gift, but rather a magical gift, because it's the one thing you want more than anything else in life. Maybe it's big, or perhaps small, or even too big to actually hold; it is your present so you can see it any way you want to.
>
> You can even hear the present. When a child is trying to figure out what is inside of a gift, they often shake it, you can even do that in your mind, hearing the gift inside of the box. Feel the shape of the box - is it square, a rectangle, or even an odd shape?
>
> And with a childlike curiosity, you can wonder what is contained in this package. Perhaps it's a winning lottery ticket...or the deed to some beautiful property, or maybe a big diamond ring...perhaps it's something even more personal to you. It belongs to you so there is no limit as you get in touch with the one thing...the one thing that you want more than anything else.
>
> And now, begin to open your gift. Remove the ribbons, the wrapping paper and lay them to the side, as you discover what it is...that thing you want SO much. Hold that gift in your hands, or lay the gift out in front of you and breathe. See your

gift, and now begin to imagine all of the changes in life as a result of getting this gift.

Notice what will change in life as a result of having this gift. How will you feel? What experiences will it bring?

Perhaps a sense of freedom? Respect of others? Will you be able to help others now that you have received this gift? Will the gift help you feel more secure, or even be more important?

Continue to explore this idea in your mind, the idea that now that you have this gift, some of your deepest needs can be met. What are they? Become aware of them. Note the words that come into your mind that describe these needs? And note the feelings you associate with this gift...

It is interesting how what we truly value or need, is often represented by an object or something tangible. In this case, your gift...and with a little reflection, we soon discover what is most important is not the gift itself, but what the gift represents.

So what you have discovered right now is actually one of your core values...that which is intrinsically important to you.

And from this moment on, from this very breath, you will find that every time you are presented with a choice in life, whether that choice has to do with what you eat or drink, or how you spend your time...you will ask yourself, "Does this choice that I am making right now bring me this gift...or does it keep me from having it?"

And in this way, you will be able to move in a valued direction in life, in a way that is congruent with your deepest values.

And as I spend time in this session with you, all of the suggestions I give you, which are actually suggestions you have asked me to make by coming here today, will help you to move towards these valued directions.

A Promise is a Promise

My clients are my best teachers and over the years, they have provided me with so many awesome ideas. One of my weight loss clients shared something she learned from Chris Powell, the well-known personal trainer from the reality television show, "Extreme Weight Loss".

This one is based on the idea that most of us are honorable folk; if we make a promise to someone else we usually do our best to uphold our word, to honor our promise. Why, then, is it so challenging to keep the promises we make to ourselves?

Here's a way to get a client moving along the road to better health by honoring themselves. I ask a client to think of one change that they can make, a relatively easy and realistic change, in the next week. This needs to be something they can maintain, that is not dependent on others, or having some special ingredients or equipment, or that takes a lot of extra time...something they can do immediately. Some of the ideas may be:

- Drink a big glass of water every morning
- Eat breakfast, even if it's just a piece of fruit
- Stand up from their desk and stretch once an hour
- Do a calming breathing exercise before they eat
- Find and cook one new healthy recipe
- Listen daily to a hypnosis recording

Of course, the best idea is the one the client comes up with, but since they have perhaps run out of solutions for themselves, they may need our creative help here.

Once your client has decided on the positive behavior, help them make a personal promise to uphold it. You can do this first verbally, having them repeat it out loud. They can write it on a piece of paper and store it in their purse or wallet. They can text it to themselves. Make it be a ritual, though, and give it the special meaning it deserves.

Once in a hypnotic state, repeat the promise-making. Add the emotion, the color, the meaning to the ritual so that it really makes an impression and then move the client through actually experiencing keeping their promise. Let them notice how they know that they are doing it, along with noticing the benefits that come with it.

Starting with just one small promise gets the things moving. A simple change that is realistic and easy to maintain provides momentum for more change; these are building blocks for making big changes in life.

Feedback from your client in your next session will tell you a lot. If they failed to keep their promise, you need to go back to the motivation well with them. If they were successful, you can harness that and compound it with more "promises".

I've had clients who actually started a "Promise Journal", gradually filling it with all of their victories along the journey. Just remember to help them keep it realistic and sustainable.

Patter Box

> *You feed your healthy, improving body foods that are delicious and nutritious.*

Chapter Five   Mindfulness for Change

State Shifting with Mindfulness

Mindfulness is a perfect path for helping people get out of unhelpful states. I often teach clients how to use a model from the RSA video, *The Secret Powers of Time*. In this example, people are described as existing in one of six places on a timeline that contains the past, the present and the future. They can be in either a positive or negative state on any of those time zones.

PAST	PRESENT	FUTURE
Pos/Neg	Pos/Neg	Pos/Neg

For example, if a person is being regretful, they are in the past in a negative state. If they are feeling nostalgic, they are in the past in a positive state. If they are anxious, worrying about what might happen, they are in the future in a negative place. If they can't wait until the weekend when they get to go to the beach, they are in the future in a positive place.

Sometimes, bad stuff is happening in the present, but for the most part, we are okay wherever we are. This timeline model can help us stay in the moment instead of suffering needlessly. Now, if a client is experiencing some uncomfortable or unhelpful mood, they can assess where on that timeline they are existing and then move themselves to one that would be more conducive to feeling better and healing better.

By keeping this time model in mind, your client can easily interrupt unhelpful mental states. And, for a client who is experiencing chronic or acute pain, being able to get out of the present moment of suffering and visit a more comfortable time and place is a wonderful thing.

And, at the very least, one can use the affirmation, "If I am breathing, I am okay," to help move through any distress and discomfort!

What is Hunger?

An interesting question to pose to most anyone is, "Are you hungry?" Watch carefully as their mind immediately conducts a transderivational search (*'The process of searching back through one's stored memories and mental representations to find the reference experience from which a current behaviour or response was derived'* Dilts, 1990) for the answer.

Some people will pause and go inside, perhaps looking for physical signs of hunger or they will access memory to recall when they last had a meal or snack and calculate whether it's time to eat again.

Many weight loss clients will stare blankly and then reply, "I never really feel hunger." Or, they will insist, "I'm always hungry!" These types of replies can be confusing, but don't worry...instead, get really excited because they are big clues that your client is going to respond well to what you are doing.

Part of our task is to wake up our clients. I've often referred to the idea that I work in the role of a "de-hypnotist", an idea which the general public finds kind of funny but also intriguing. When it comes to helping our weight loss clients awaken, it's a matter of opening the door to better communication between mind and body – and this is a particular forte for hypnotists who, after all, are mind-body experts.

Regardless of how a client answers my, "Are you hungry?" question, I am going to make sure that they learn some essential stuff that includes:

- What physical hunger is and feels like
- What emotional hunger is and feels like
- How to distinguish between the two hungers
- How to respond effectively to each

When a client fails to know if they are hungry for food or not, I simply ask them to place their hand on their stomach and "listen" – I explain that they can listen with their ears or they can listen with their hand. It may help to close their eyes, especially if they are feeling self-conscious; after all, they are bringing their attention (and mine) to a very vulnerable part of the body, the belly.

Note: Don't be surprised if your client doesn't initially know where their stomach is. They may put their hand on their lower abdomen or up on their chest, so help them find the location of their stomach without touching. The best method is to demonstrate on yourself.

It's vital to be patient here, so let your client sit for a while, paying attention to how this feels. After a bit, I offer an idea, saying,

> *If Zero feels like a really empty stomach...and 10 is a feeling of being so full that you can't eat another bite...where are you on that scale?*

They will usually respond fairly quickly. I'll even share my own hunger rating, explaining that I ate a meal recently so I'm aware that I'm feeling satisfied and don't need to eat for quite some time. Or, if it's been a while, I'll observe that I'll be ready to eat a healthy meal within a few hours.

Waking a client back up to listening to those internal signals of physical satiation or hunger is important so I will encourage them to identify exactly what they feel like. If a client is noticing some hunger signs, I will ask them to explain; perhaps they notice a feeling of emptiness or a little gnawing sensation.

And, of course, not all symptoms of physical hunger occur in the stomach: many people start to feel fatigued or can feel dizziness and even irritation as blood sugar levels dip. Help your client identify the signs that they individually experience, even writing them down on paper. Point out that their body has always been communicating with these signals and this is a powerful example of how they have been effectively able to "tune" them out!

Ironically, some of the people who struggle with being overweight or obese have become so successful at ignoring physical hunger signs that they fail to eat breakfast, sometimes going for extended periods of time without sustenance. They then conclude their day with large amounts of food, binging or grazing throughout the

67

evening. Or, they actually eat a small amount overall, usually nutrient-light foods, and have, over time, effectively disabled their metabolism.

This simple demonstration, along with showing a version of a Hunger Scale (see the Appendix at the end of this book) can be a compelling part of raising awareness. Of course, learning new things is just part of the journey – using the knowledge and applying it is what makes the difference, so I ask a client, "Can you imagine the power of checking in with your body...whenever you think that you may need to eat?"

Or, in the case of a client who just doesn't eat enough, "Can you imagine, with your hand...there, that your stomach and your body is asking to receive consistent, regular amounts of healthy food?"

I can't tell you how many clients return for a subsequent appointment and announce, "I check in with my body before eating!"

Patter Box

> *Your body is the vehicle of your life...and you are now taking better care of it in all ways.*

Emotional Eating

This leads us to the topic of another type of hunger altogether: emotional hunger. Most people are familiar with this concept and may even mention early on to you that they are emotional "eaters". And while some may profess not to be influenced by their emotions, I have noticed that since all humans do experience emotions, it's virtually impossible to have an absence of emotions before, during or after an eating experience! Even if it's a sense of anticipation, or pleasure, or satisfaction...our inner senses are involved to some degree.

For those who are motivated to eat not merely from the need to re-fuel their physical body, it's helpful to identify how emotions may be triggering poor eating choices.

I start with asking a client to identify which emotions "make" them eat in unhealthy ways. (As hypnosis practitioners, we understand that nothing and no one can actually cause a person to react a certain way; they are at some level choosing that reaction.)

I clarify that I am asking about inappropriate eating behavior, that which is causing them to retain the excess weight. Perhaps a client notices that they eat inappropriately when they are stressed, or they eat too much at night, when they are bored...or lonely. We list these triggering emotions and then discuss what these emotions are about and what they are trying to communicate, along with possible ways the client can respond, instead of just eating.

Along with identifying those triggering emotions, I will ask a client to notice where in their body they feel the specific emotion. Not surprisingly, a majority of weight loss clients indicate sensations in the throat or the gut area. This is a good opportunity to introduce the idea of the Second Brain or the Abdominal Brain, better known as our enteric nervous system.

Our enteric nervous system contains our digestive tract, which is a pretty complex thing, considering all that it does. From the moment when a person first sees or even thinks about a food choice, the appropriate taste buds are firing off and preparing for the digestive process. Science has been able to determine that because this process is so complex, so very detailed in function, it needs a management system. And that system is contained within the cells that line the digestive tract, cells that are very similar to the same ones that reside deep in the brain, in the hypothalamus gland. These cells help to process and regulate our emotions.

Think about it: the cells lining our digestive tract know how to respond to emotional triggers! People who are emotional eaters are thrilled to hear this because it finally explains not only the sensations they have been experiencing, it explains why they have been trying to eat to satisfy their emotions. And those whose appetites shut down when they are emotionally taxed understand the havoc that response creates with digestion in general.

Of course, all of us are individuals and so we all physically react differently when it comes to emotional triggers. Some people mistake that cell activation in the gut as a hunger signal while others feel nauseated. Some people get a lump in the throat and can't swallow. Some people get constipated while others get diarrhea.

Many weight-challenged clients think that they need to eat and then can't understand why they never really feel full, despite the fact that their stomach is probably ready to bust! So this bit of key information can begin to help them question what it is that they really hunger for and then find the proper response for that need.

Being able to distinguish when they are hungry for food, rather than being hungry for some emotional need, is really, really important when it comes to attending properly to signals. I teach my clients to, when they think they need to eat something, look down (distracting themselves from the outside world), place their hand on their stomach and ask themselves, "What am I really hungry for?" If they find they are needing some emotional sustenance, they can look up and think of a proper response that will satisfy that emotion.

If they discover that they really are hungry for food, they can assess the hunger level and decide if they need to eat soon or if they can wait a while. They can then decide on a healthy and delicious choice to satisfy that physical hunger.

There are several distinct differences between physical hunger and emotional hunger and I discuss these with my clients, using a version of a handout from Doreen Virtue, "Constant Craving A-Z". My version of it is on the following page.

This is information I usually address in a second session with my client. During the intake, I have asked them to share any emotional triggers to unhealthy eating and while I relieve them of the task of having to journal their food choices, I do ask them to notice what mood they are in when eating and present that to me at the next session. This provides a nice introduction to the whole topic of emotional eating and gives the client a better handle on what is happening, including some ways to get control of it.

Emotional Hunger	Physical Hunger
1. Is sudden; comes on quickly and without warning.	1. Is gradual and takes time to build. You can wait a while to eat.
2. Is for a specific food. You crave chocolate, burgers, cake, etc. and you will not settle for any other food.	2. Will be satisfied with pretty much any food choice and is open to eating a wider variety of foods.
3. Is based "above the neck". Food cravings are imagined in the mind, experienced in the mouth and nose.	3. Is felt primarily in the stomach region, in the form of sensations of emptiness, gnawing or even pain.
4. Is urgent. Emotional hunger urges you to EAT NOW in an effort to ease whatever emotion is upsetting and bothering you.	4. Is patient. You can certainly wait some time before eating your next meal or snack and you can take time to plan it.
5. Arrives with an upsetting emotion. This can be an actual event but it can also come from just *thinking* about a difficult situation or relationship.	5. Comes from a physical need for fuel: the energy levels are being depleted. It's been some time since you ate and your body needs to be re-energized.
6. Involves mindless eating; awareness of the type and quantity of food being consumed is absent. It can even feel like *someone else* is eating it!	6. Pays attention to the eating process. Enjoys and savors food choices and is aware of becoming full, stopping when you've had enough.
7. Does not notice or stop eating in response to fullness. The satiation mechanism doesn't work properly and you continue to eat, despite having had plenty.	7. Understands and attends to the signal that the body has received enough food, being able to stop eating when satisfied and feeling good about that.
8. Feels guilt, regret and other unhelpful emotions after eating. This, of course, can lead to even more inappropriate eating!	8. Understands that eating food is not only necessary, it can be pleasurable. There is no guilt or shame when providing the body with the proper nutrition in the right quantities.

You may be noticing how important it is to help a client gain awareness of what is driving their weight issues, along with helping them find solutions. Very often, failing to pay enough attention is the culprit...

Patter Box

> *Imagine how GOOD it can feel the more you start to nourish those deeper parts of you...You can...and the more you do...notice...how things start to shift inside of you...Find how so much better you can fill that space inside with what REALLY nourishes your body, heart and mind!*
>
> ~ Marina Makuchev

Mindful Eating and Drinking

Much of the problem with overweight clients lies in how they eat food; their relationship with food is shallow. They fail to pay close attention not only to what they are eating, but the eating process itself. That's a shame, because when we eat without regard, we miss out on the actual pleasure that food can provide.

During your client assessment, you probably discovered some of the habits that were contributing to the weight issues, such as eating too much, eating too quickly, or eating while standing, driving or otherwise occupied. Of course, awareness of these details starts the change ball rolling and some clients, once aware of problematic behavior, are able to self-correct.

But more often, they need our help and one of the first behaviors that I target for change is that positional one: I ask a client to always be sitting when eating, preferably at a clean table or counter. I suggest that they set the dining area with a nice tablecloth or mat, use their real dishes (not disposable) and even add a candle or flowers to the scene. They are encouraged to use a beautiful glass for their water.

Surprisingly often, at this point, a client will reveal that they don't have any space on their kitchen counter or dining table for actual eating! Think about what we are doing for a client as helping them work on their own personal feng shui – if their living conditions have terrible feng shui, it's going to be more challenging for them to create inner balance. It's not uncommon to have clutter and even hoarding issues related to obesity so it's a good idea to have some tactics in mind; at the very least a resource you can refer them to for help in de-cluttering their living environment.

I also ask a client to turn off the television and put aside any reading materials. Helping a person make the eating ritual a pleasant one creates a more mindful atmosphere and that's what we're going for.

In the meantime, we want to quickly plant ideas for mindful eating and drinking that will help create some immediate improvements. I usually use this simple approach in a first session with a weight loss client:

Few Bites

I'd like you to imagine that you are at a place of dining. It may be at home, or it could be out at a restaurant or some other place. Wherever you decide, you are there alone...and in front of you is your favorite food. Imagine that you are there, now.

Take some time to really notice your favorite food there. Be like a gourmet and pay attention to the presentation...the colors...the textures...any aromas...notice everything that you love about this favorite food. Please pay attention in particular to how this food makes you feel emotionally.

PAUSE

Now, go ahead, take a bite of your favorite food. Notice the anticipation, right before you put it into your mouth...the excitement, the pending pleasure. And...as you feel it in your mouth, the textures, the explosion of delicious flavors...as you begin to chew it, slowly...noticing all that you can notice...

Notice what thoughts come to mind as you chew your favorite food. Notice how it feels in your mouth...how you feel about this experience of eating your favorite food. Be sure to chew it thoroughly and when you are ready, go ahead and swallow.

PAUSE

That's right...now, take a second bite of your favorite food. Notice, once again, how it feels...how it makes you feel...as you chew it...

PAUSE

...and swallow. And, another bite...

PAUSE

...and another...

PAUSE

And you are already getting the idea...you are already getting the picture...that it's just the first few bites of food that gives you that pleasure...that impact...that enjoyment...and those effects begin to quickly fade...

And when you realize this...when you KNOW this...it becomes so much easy to enjoy smaller amount of food...in fact, I don't know if you ate half of that favorite food...or less than half...But you are satisfied...You feel full...Half is plenty...less is more...you feel good.

See what is left there in front of you...Place your hands next to that food and push it away...Notice how great that feels to take control of your eating...To enjoy less and feel full...

You can always save the rest of that food for another meal...that's fine...or, you can throw it away...that's okay, too.

There is always enough food...you will never run out of food...If you were to eat it, it would just turn to waste, anyway!

Pushing the rest of that food away...feeling good about your choice to take control of your eating...You are in control and you are already feeling better...

From here you can continue on to future pacing, post hypnotic suggestions, etc. This brief process is very effective and helps enormously in the area of volume control for problem eating. Many clients remark later that they actually "tried to eat" all of their favorite food at some point following this experience and found it impossible! What a convincer!

Patter Box

> *Less is more...half is plenty!*
>
> *It feels so good to be in control...enjoying smaller amount of food in greater ways...*

Clients love to hear about little tricks that help them eat smaller amounts. For example, the color blue is an appetite depressant (unless you happen to live in Italy, where the color of the national soccer team is *azure*!) so eating off a blue plate can reduce the volume you consume. So can eating with a large fork – weird, huh?

I've put together a small dining set for my weight loss clients, stocking up on small plates and bowls from IKEA. They only cost a few dollars and when presented with the suggestion that using them will create weight loss, make a powerful tool for change. Clients do appreciate extras like this, too, and will respond by sending me photos of healthy meals they are enjoying with the dishes.

Another way that I help a client get in touch with feelings of satiety is to use this exercise that I picked up along the way (my apologies, I don't recall the source):

A Full Cup

Materials need: 1 Solo cup, 8-10 paper towel sheets that are wadded up into balls

Hand the Solo cup to your client. Tell them to imagine that the cup is their stomach. Have them keep their eyes open, as the visual effect of this exercise is important.

Begin to hand your client the paper towel balls, one at a time, asking them to place them in the cup. The cup will quickly fill. Continue to pass the balls to the client, so that they need to start compressing, pushing and otherwise fitting them into the cup.

They quickly get the idea. That cup is filled to overflowing and at some point, there just is no more room for more paper towel balls. I then ask them, "How does that feel to you?" They clearly understand the correlation between over eating and that stuffed Solo cup.

I ask them, "When was the last time that you ate so much...you felt like that?" We can explore and discuss how that happened and how it felt to them. We can also remove some of the paper balls to a level that would be a reasonable volume, allowing the client to learn that it's okay to eat smaller amounts, paying attention as they do.

In fact, I will mention that they can visualize the Solo cup, quickly filling, the next time that they eat, so that they can better judge when to stop eating. One client started using Solo cups to measure her portion sizes, which was counter-productive when it came to her "goodies". I encouraged her to instead use it for salads, fruit and veggies.

So, while using visual imagery to effect behavioral change is really effective, using props is, too. To promote mindful eating, I keep a container of fresh yellow raisins on hand and offer one on a tiny silver platter to my client...using Roger's Raisin Meditation process:

Raisin Meditation (credit: Roger Moore)

> *Bring your attention to the raisin...observing it carefully as if you had never seen one before. Touch the raisin with a finger. Is it rough...or smooth? Thick or thin? Hard or soft? Feel its texture between your fingers...Feel the weight of it and notice its colors.*
>
> *Be aware of any thoughts you might be having about the raisin. Note any thoughts or feelings of liking or disliking raisins. Notice the color...the topography of the raisin... look into the valleys and the peaks...the highlights and the dark crevasses.*
>
> *Lift the raisin to your nose and smell the fragrance...what does it remind you of?*
>
> *Close your eyes and bring the raisin to your lips, being aware of the arm moving the hand to position it correctly and of your mouth begin to salivate in anticipation of receiving the raisin...feel the emptiness inside your mouth.*
>
> *Take the raisin into your mouth and just allow it to sit there for a moment. Do not chew it...slowly move it around with your tongue...as the raisin lays in your mouth...notice if the raisin is warm or cool...notice the texture, the rough edges and the smooth surfaces...and the flavor...notice the subtleties of the flavor.*
>
> *Hold the raisin between your teeth and now bite down once into it...notice the sweetness...the sound...notice your thoughts and reactions...your emotions...notice your breathing. As you separate your teeth...now what do you*

notice? Note how the texture changes as you begin to chew the raisin...becoming aware of the temperature of it, the juiciness of it...

Do not swallow yet...and allow yourself to become aware of how that feels...to not swallow...

Slowly, finish chewing the raisin and when the raisin is all but dissolved...go ahead and swallow.

Can you imagine enjoying other foods in this manner? Giving yourself time to really appreciated all of the nuances of food, chewing your food thoroughly, slowly?

Patter Box

> *Before you decide to eat anything...stop and take a nice deep breath into the center of yourself and ask...what will make me feel happy and healthy and satisfied 30 minutes from now? ...and whatever you choose to eat...enjoy it completely...with no negative self talk.... eat it slowly, savoring every delicious bite...and simply stop when you feel full with this new wonderful sense of satisfaction...*
> ~Sally Homes Reed

Mindful Drinking

Something that presents often in our practices, whether it's related to weight issues or not, is problematic alcohol drinking. A client might confess that they indulge in more alcohol on a regular basis than they know is good for them or that they want to. But, they may not want to give up the practice entirely and simply want to moderate it. This is something that is relatively easy for us to help them with, providing they are being honest with themselves and with you. If it becomes apparent that your client has a bigger problem, you can help them do a self-assessment and give them a referral for proper treatment.

Note: I do not work with people who have more than a dependency on alcohol, partly because this is legally beyond my scope of practice but also because until a person admits that they need some serious help, they are likely to be less committed to our work and I never want to work harder than my client! In the rare case that somewhere along the program, it becomes clear that alcohol is a big problem, I suggest that the client seek out appropriate help and that I will be there to augment it or that we can pick up on our sessions when they have a bit more stability.

That personal guideline being said, moderate drinking is something that many people can do. Adding mindfulness to it can help control it, curb it and even stop it during the weight loss process, if desired by the client. This is really important, so I will repeat: if desired by the client. Be sure this is what your client wants. Just like when helping someone stop smoking tobacco, we need to follow their wishes if they want to retain a pot-smoking habit...we need to get specifics about how and when a person wants to enjoy alcohol.

Of course, merely by addressing some of the negative emotional and situational influences in a client's life, they will notice a reduction in their need and desire to use alcohol and that's great. But follow your client's lead when creating suggestions about alcohol consumption because if you do not, it can set up deceptive reactions and add to feelings of guilt, hurting your effectiveness with them.

One approach that I use in cases where a person wants to limit their alcohol use is to introduce them to mindful drinking. Just like with eating, drinking a cocktail or a glass of wine can be a pleasant experience, especially when one is fully engaged with it and not just gulping it down in a distracted manner.

Pay particular attention to the why, how, when and where of your client's drinking activity. For best results, teach them how to really be engaged – that means turning off the television or computer.

Here's my mindful drinking script – adjust it to suit your client's preferences and needs:

Let's begin with closing your eyes and taking a couple of relaxing breaths...notice how your body begins to immediately relax as you do that. Good.

Now, please imagine, in your mind's eye, that you have just settled down for the evening. Maybe you are there by yourself, maybe your family/partner is there with you. Whatever is going on, notice that you are unwinding, looking forward to the rest of the night. And, as you have learned, part of that relaxing time involves enjoying an alcoholic beverage. (Pick beverage of choice)

See and feel yourself there, now. You get your favorite glass...you feel the weight of it in your hand. You set it down, you get the alcohol and you slowly, carefully pour a serving into your glass. As you do, you notice the color of the liquid, the motion of it, the light of it...maybe an aroma.

Become aware of how you are feeling...any emotions...or sensations...a sense of expectation...or anticipation...

Now, you pick up the glass and you notice how it feels...the weight of it now, with the drink in it. You can notice the temperature of the glass...Perhaps you swirl the liquid around, watching as it moves inside the glass, the shape of it changing...Take some time to appreciate the colors, the textures of the liquid...and also notice any thoughts or emotions that surface...without judging them...just notice them...

And now, bring the glass up to your nose...breathe in the fragrance of the beverage...Notice how that feels...how you react to that smell...

Bring the glass to your mouth and feel it against your lips. As you do this, pause...not drinking yet...but noticing how it feels and what thoughts and emotions you experience as you interrupt that automatic tendency to sip...

80

When you are ready, take a sip. Hold it in your mouth, swirl it around without swallowing. Focus on the sensations and the feelings that arise.

Finally, go ahead and swallow the liquid...with intention. Become aware of how that feels and what that means to you and about you that you are doing this.

You can use the above meditation in hypnosis with a client, having them imagine the drinking experience, or you can actually involve them in it experientially by providing water or actual alcohol (obviously, use discretion with the latter).

Another successful tactic to help limit alcohol consumption involves future pacing the client with their beverage of choice, drinking mindfully, and then moving them to the next glass...that is filled with water or perhaps sparkling water. Provide the experience of how drinking subsequent glasses of water *feels* good to them and gives them all of the same benefits, if not better, that the old way of drinking did.

Layer in the positive results that come from having made this change, allowing them to once again experience the weight loss and any other improvements that drinking less alcohol brings. I might even suggest that some unexpected, wonderful benefit has arrived as a result of having made these changes!

Patter Box

Water is quickly becoming your favourite beverage...in fact, when you enjoy a refreshing serving of water, you feel your mind and your body respond delightfully!

Time Distortion

The next time you are dining out, look around and notice the rate of speed at which people consume their food and beverage. Can you notice a correlation between how fast they eat and their body size? Research suggests that fast eaters are more than twice as likely to be obese compared to those who eat slowly.

Part of the reason for this is that it can take up to 20 minutes for the brain to get the message that enough food has been consumed. Most fast eaters who are heavy eat excess quantities, especially if they are not paying attention while watching television or engaging in some other distraction.

Additionally, gulping down your food also raises the risk for these undesirable effects:

- Higher insulin resistance
- Up to 2.5 times more likely to have diabetes
- Metabolic syndrome
- Poor digestion – gut issues
- Less overall satisfaction and satiety

I've worked with a fair amount of clients who have a military background and they often have in common the habit of wolfing down meals. When in the service, they usually only had a limited amount of time to eat so they made the most of it. Later, no longer as physically active, that type of eating contributed to weight gain.

Some clients who were raised with large families who had financial struggles also report that they learned how to "race" to get enough food. Helping these clients update how their Inner Child is eating is usually required.

I've used mindfulness and hypnotic time distortion to help slow down a client's eating behaviour. Depending on the individual, challenging them to be the *last* person at the table to finish their meal can also help, especially when they are the only one who knows what they are doing.

Nightly Grazing

A common complaint weight loss clients share is that they find themselves eating during the evening hours, after they have enjoyed a full meal and often throughout the night, until they go to bed.

As mentioned, emotional states may be contributing to this behaviour and physical ones certainly need to be considered and addressed. (I discuss how to help a client be more physically comfortable during these times later in this book.)

There are some effective tactics we can utilize to help people stop these nightly foraging and feeding activities. Again, these are often engrained habits that need to be interrupted and re-wired. Here are some ideas:

Create a Food Free Zone

Eating activity has gradually over the decades moved out of the former designations of kitchens, dining areas and sit-down restaurants. There are practically no restrictions on the places, times and situations where eating is allowed and even encouraged.

We eat in our cars, we eat in classrooms, we eat in airplanes and on trains. We eat in bed, in front of the television or at the computer and most unhealthfully, we eat on the run. We eat all over the place and often all of the time and because of this we have lost touch with the absolute beauty and pace of eating for enjoyment and good health.

Some of us have been fortunate enough to experience a leisurely meal in a European style, with course after course served amid interesting conversation and plenty of time for savouring the food. But many people would find impatience for this, having entrained their minds and bodies for the quickest, most convenient eating tactics possible.

With this in mind, consider encouraging your client to establish a "Food Free Zone". This can be comprised of making a room or rooms in their home sacrosanct, where no eating will occur. Create a metaphorical barrier or blockade to food, with a symbolic key that your client is able to access and use.

Be sure to bring in positive, helpful resources when you do – we don't want this space to be a prison cell! I have helped clients establish a place in their home where they can indulge in uplifting and helpful experiences such as using self-hypnosis, listening to music, creating art, learning and even having great sex. You can think of this approach as effectively crowding out unhealthy eating behaviours with other, better activities.

A Food Free Zone can also consist of time parameters. Lots of people eat fairly well throughout their busy day and it's only when night time arrives that they find themselves reeling out of control. One of the ways that I successfully let go of weight was to eat like my parents – having dinner early in the evening and not eating after 6 pm, on most days.

Let your client choose what those Food Free time zones will be and help them create anchors for moving into them. One such anchor that works well is tooth brushing. Setting up a behaviour such as brushing teeth at a certain hour moves a person into non-eating mode easily. The ritual of brushing teeth can also be associated to self-love processes when looking in the mirror. I offer some of these in the following chapter.

Patter Box

> *There's always something better to do than eat _____.*

Chapter Six   Ego Strengthening

Not every overweight or obese person suffers from low self-esteem and I've met several who are comfortable in their own skin and enjoy life. More often, though, those who seek out our help are motivated for change due to the way excess weight drags down their physical comfort, spirits and self-regard, especially since we live in a culture that is based so much upon appearance.

For these clients, whose friends or family members may assure them that they are loved and valued, it is hard for them to believe that they are worthy of love and acceptance. This creates a terrible cycle of self-destruction through eating to try to feel better, which is then followed by regret and recriminations, leading to even more unhealthy eating.

Many people who struggle with being overweight think, "Oh, if only I lose the weight...THEN I'll be happy."

My take on this is, "Why wait? Get happy now and watch the weight adjust."

I have found that if we can promote a sense of well-being and in particular, a sense of self-love and respect, our clients will automatically begin to improve their food choices. As Michael Ellner is prone to say, "People who feel better, heal better!" I know that as soon as my clients start relaxing and feeling happier, they also start taking better care of themselves.

Patter Box

A body and mind that is nourished, flourishes. ~ Leslie Teltoe

I created a hypnotic experience to help clients who are not used to being in the spotlight of their own affection and may even feel that taking care of themselves is selfish. In fact, that's exactly what I named it and it goes something like this:

Spotlight of Unconditional Positive Regard

Imagine that in your hand you hold a spotlight device of some kind. Lift it up and turn it on. We do have the amazing ability to turn our attention toward someone or something, don't we?

See that light shine from your device now...shining on a particular target. Perhaps it's a person you care for, maybe it's a family member or a friend. Or it may be shining on some aspect of your work or your home. Really take some time to notice how clearly you can see and experience the details of this...observing this target of your Spotlight of Attention. Good...

Now imagine that there are more than just one of these spotlights. See them hovering at arm's reach, almost like a panel of spotlights and notice that both of your hands are busy now, turning on these lights, aiming them at specific targets, in different directions. As you become aware of all of the people, the places, the things in your life that are important to you, that demand your attention.

You may even designate certain colors of spotlights for these various targets. What color would you shine on loved ones? What color represents your work, your passions...your interests? What color suits the less pleasant tasks or responsibilities? Notice the many spotlights, the many colors...notice the amount of effort it takes to juggle them, to coordinate and control them.

When there are so many demands for our attention and our affection, it can become overwhelming and draining to us. As a result, we can feel exhausted, lacking in energy and well-being. Our emotional states are worn down and our physical states start to break down. We neglect self-care and even feel guilty about making time for ourselves, whether it is to read a book or take a bath...or even to get a good night's sleep!

What I want you to do now... is to turn off those spotlights. That's right, just reach up and, one at a time, turn off those spotlights...click, click, click. They will be there for you when you need to turn them on again. Turn all of them off...except for just one. Leave just one spotlight on, please.

When you are ready, notice this one, special spotlight. It is casting a brilliant, golden light out in a beam directly in front of you. As you become more and more aware of this golden spotlight, I want you to notice that someone is walking into it. Someone who is very important to you is now standing, right in the center of this spotlight. And that someone is...you.

See yourself now...standing in this brilliant, golden spotlight and understand that this light comes from a source with you – it is the source of unconditional love, the source of acceptance and forgiveness. You can even imagine that you see yourself standing in the Spotlight of Affection. You can see yourself, your true self, deserving of love, deserving of kindness, of being taken care of. What do you need to tell yourself that will allow you to accept all of that? What do you notice about yourself that is wonderful? Go ahead, tell yourself anything that you need to hear, that you want to hear, that you deserve to hear at this time...

Good...Now, I want you to see yourself there in that light, reaching out. You can take your hand and allow yourself to be gently, sweetly pulled into...yourself. So that now, you are there, standing in the warm, loving glow of your Spotlight of Affection. Let yourself experience all of that unconditional love, all of that acceptance...all of that affection. Know that you deserve this, that you are now able to accept and enjoy loving and caring for yourself.

From this point on and every day, you can stand in the loving light of your Spotlight of Affection and let it wash away any unwelcome, unhelpful thoughts, feelings, impressions and allow it to fill you with wonderful, supportive ideas and emotions. This will help remind you to keep your life in balance and you realize that when you are well, when you are feeling right with yourself, you are better able to shine your loving affection onto others.

Patter Box

> *I love myself enough not to punish myself with eating poorly as I am worth more than that!* ~ Susan McElligott

TIP: Add post hypnotic suggestion that when the client is doing some daily habit, such as preparing to brush their teeth, awareness of this Spotlight of Affection will arrive.

Self-Talk

Let us talk about self-talk. You may know it as that inner voice that gives feedback, either in our own voice or sometimes in someone else's. Self-talk is neither bad nor good, it just is. And when we take the time to listen and examine not only the messages we are interpreting from these thoughts but the origin of them, it becomes easier to direct them in more helpful ways.

For example, one client, as he was departing from our initial hypnosis session and I said, "Next time, I'll see less of you!" replied, "We'll see..." Of course, I had to stop him and help him attend to his own language. He was shocked to recall that "We'll see..." was the exact same thing his own doubting father had repeatedly told him, whenever he was taking on a challenge.

For me, that gentleman's phrase resonated at about 3 on the Hope Scale and about 2 on the Belief Scale – not too helpful! After realizing how his father's words were potentially limiting him, my client decided to release them, then and there.

Another phrase that often comes out of people's mouths is, "I'll try." I understand that using these words allows us to keep a back door open for an easy escape. When I hear a client say that to me about one of their goals or even a promise they are making to themselves, I immediately say, "Wow. What if I had said to you, when you called me and made this appointment, 'I'll try to be there.' - How would you have felt about that?"

We want to get full-out commitment from our clients, so it's vital that we help them identify and adjust any of these limiting voices. Even if they don't fully believe what they are thinking and saying, that's okay. I explain that the part of their mind that we are targeting doesn't care about reality or pretense – it can play with either!

Cultivating Sisu

"Strong willpower will take a woman even through stone."

~ Finnish proverb

Driving in town one day, I noticed a bumper sticker on a work van ahead. It asked, "GOT SISU?" I smiled because I do have sisu. It's actually part of my Finnish ancestry.

"Sisu" (see-su) is a Finnish word that describes an element of Finnish culture which represents a dogged perseverance. To the Finnish people, "sisu" has a nearly mystical, magical aura, bordering on the spiritual.

"The Finns have something they call sisu. It is a compound of bravado and bravery, of ferocity and tenacity, of the ability to keep fighting after most people would have quit, and to fight with the will to win. The Finns translate sisu as "the Finnish spirit," but it is a much more gutful word than that. Last week the Finns gave the world a good example of sisu by carrying the war into Russian territory on one front while on another they withstood merciless attacks by a reinforced Russian Army. In the wilderness that forms most of the Russo-Finnish frontier between Lake Laatokka and the Arctic Ocean, the Finns definitely gained the upper hand."

~ Time Magazine, January 8, 1940

I started thinking about my own sisu nature and realized that this is the element that I often seek to instill in my clients. While they may not be in a war against an invading country, they ARE involved in a battle within and need all of the reserves we can muster. Casting a powerful force like sisu can help them navigate the trenches and persevere to the completion of their goals.

Creating Power Signals

If words create imagery and imagery creates not only emotional but physical responses, then it only makes sense to use powerful words to create powerful responses in our weight loss clients. I learned a nifty process from Marc Savard that allows a client to choose a specific word (or maybe the word chooses *them*) and turn it into a Power Signal.

With Marc's permission, I've customized and used this approach for years for clients whose chronic issues have left them feeling disempowered. Imagine making it even more personal when you add terminology that really resonates with your client!

Preface this exercise by telling your client that what you are going to do will increase their confidence in being able to use their mind to help them feel better, which will make their weight loss even more effective. You will be offering a series of words and you want them to listen to each word, allow themselves to notice how the word feels to them, how it affects them. Tell the client to "try the word on and see if it fits you" or otherwise resonates with their nervous system. When a word (or words) speaks to them, they will remember it...

Then, begin to slowly and steadily recite each of the words on your list. Repeat each word three times. Keep a consistent tone and pace. Observe your client as they experience the words, looking for clues about how they respond to them.

Once you have completed the list of words, ask your client to remember the word that really spoke to them. Have them repeat it in their mind and notice how it feels as the word rolls across their nervous system. Bring their attention to the feelings that are invoked by the word, where they feel this in their body, etc.

Next, tell your client that you are going to help them turn this "Power Word" into a Power Signal, so that they may tap into it whenever they want to, whenever they need to.

Instruct your client to repeat their word three times, noticing how it feels to bring in all of the characteristics of the word. You can use a patter like this:

> Staying focused, relaxed, repeat your power word, repeat it three times. Whenever you hear this word, you will feel the word.
>
> Say to yourself,
> *"Whenever I think this word, I will become this word."*
> *"Whenever I hear this word, I will become this word."*
> *"Whenever I see this word, I will become this word."*
>
> Imagine yourself going through your day, being this word. See yourself at home, with family, at play. When you think the word, whenever you see or say the word, you become it.

You can further anchor the Power Signal with some Post-It notes or some other physical reminder. I have a supply of smooth stones that are engraved with Power Words and clients are always amazed when, following this exercise, I hand them one with their own word.

Here's a suggested Power Word list to get you started. Be sure to include any words that your client has already shared with you as having special meaning.

peace	bright	beautiful	joy	comfort
clear	complete	healthy	bliss	blooming
strength	glory	radiant	love	gratitude
calming	wonderful	focused	happy	nutritious

faith	unlimited	forgiven	firm	grounded
enough	confident	proud	free	unshakeable
majestic	releasing	breathe	plenty	compassion
amazing	blessed	splendid	okay	remarkable

Releasing Limiting Imprints

Weight loss client are often carrying outdated or otherwise unhelpful imprints and impressions, some from childhood, others collected along the way as they move through life. These usually surface in one way or another; even during the intake process a client may provide clues about specific beliefs or thoughts that are not congruent with their current desire to be healthier.

An example of that may be when a client remarks that all of the women in her family gain weight as they get older, or that a parent used to force them to finish all of the food on their plate.

While discussing these thoughts can be helpful, raising awareness, when we have a clinical conversation about the need to eat proper amounts of healthy food and the harmful effects of over-eating, the subconscious is basically snoring with boredom. But, when we approach limiting thoughts from a hypnotic perspective, we get its attention not only because we have moved into a very focused trance state but because we elicit emotive modalities that involve all of the senses.

I've taken an idea first created by one of my amazing friends, Nathan Welch, who is a family and child therapist in England, and adjusted it for use with weight loss clients. Guiding a client through it provides opportunity to release limiting imprints and beliefs, while encouraging the discovery and utilization of inner strengths and resources. This is a dynamic, fluid experience that starts with the listener observing themselves in a full length mirror as they currently are and inviting any thoughts or emotions related to that vision to surface. Since it's usually pretty common for us to notice our flaws, this means some of those may be negative and that's alright!

We don't linger there long, though, but move into noticing how we may be carrying (wearing) things that are outdated, ill-fitting, scratchy or otherwise uncomfortable (limitations). Perhaps we personally chose those things or maybe they were put upon us...even before we realized it or knew any better.

I invite the listener to take these unnecessary, unwanted things off and hand them back, through the mirror, to their original source. This is done in an open context and doesn't require that those sources are even consciously recognized. Using these metaphors automatically engages the subconscious, which is holding on to those limitations.

Following this, awareness is given of a beautiful wardrobe, a closet of their own design, just adjacent to the mirror. Into this we delve for garments, accessories and props of CHOICE. (Being in choice is preferable to being in control!) I expand on the possible selection and let the listener make the choices...choices which represent traits, abilities, attitudes and emotions that are more congruent with who they are and who they wish to be.

I then future pace the listener into a time when they are "wearing" items from the Wardrobe of Wonder, guiding them in using these inner resources to handle challenges and generally improve their lives. I further suggest they can return to it anytime to update their selections, since we are always changing!

As with all of my scripts, use the following as a template and allow your client to provide the inspiration for customization:

Wardrobe of Wonder

Begin by taking a nice, deep breath. We can always use our breath and our awareness of our breath as a cue to enter a different state of being...no matter what is going on around us...when we just breathe a little deeper and longer, some interesting things begin to happen...one of which is that we give ourselves permission to turn inward...and inward is where we go when we take a hypnotic journey...

So, just breathing easily now and, if it's safe for you, I wonder if you would even like to close your eyes for a while...this makes it even easier to engage the creative imagination, that realm within your subconscious where anything is possible...that's right

And I'd like you to imagine that you are standing now...in front of a full length mirror...perhaps it's like a mirror you have at home, or it may be somewhere else...it's your mirror so you can design it however you wish...

And as you do, notice the reflection of yourself in this mirror...yourself as you are currently...it may have appeared spontaneously or it may be a bit vague...you can always look to see what you are wearing upon your feet...or perhaps they are bare...as you develop this image, you can start to become aware of what you are wearing or even carrying...sometimes we think we wear certain things by choice when the truth is that often, choices are made for us before we are even aware of it.

So...look now...and see...are there some things that are outdated...ill-fitting...maybe even constrictive or scratchy? Do they clash with each other...or with you? Are there some items that you have been wearing for a long time that just don't suit who you are or who you want to be?

This is your chance now to remove these things...just take them off...that's right...unbutton, unzip, peel these unwanted, outdated things off...and then...just hand them back...right through that mirror...you can hand them back from whence they came...just give them back...you don't need them anymore! Notice how good that feels to take them off and let go of them...that's right...

And now I want you to notice...that right next to the mirror, off to the side, is a closet...a wardrobe...a wardrobe of wonder...that is filled with an unlimited selection of marvelous, uplifting, inspiring, nurturing items...and they are all available to you. Perhaps they are hanging or maybe they are folded nicely...or rolled and tucked into cubbies, waiting to be discovered. Some colors jump out at you, textures invite your touch...there are even fantastic aromas coming from this wardrobe.

So go ahead...try something on! Do you want to feel more confident? Look what's there for you! When you put those on your feet you feel on top of the world!

Perhaps you prefer some romance...an intimate garment or accessory softens and melts you...

How would you dress to meet a challenge? With a cape...or maybe some special glasses that allow you to see solutions instead of obstacles?

If you are suffering a loss...can you find a momento, a piece of jewelry or some other item that helps you move past the grief while filling you with positive memories?

And, what would you like to wear or use that will enhance your weight loss journey? Can you find something there that will help you?

Play for a while...look, touch, smell, listen...notice that the contents of your wardrobe IS unlimited...limited only by your imagination, which is limitless. You can return here on your own anytime you wish and try on some new ideas, some new habits, abilities and attitudes and then carry them out into your world, noticing the difference!

When you're ready...open your eyes and return to the here and now, taking a wonderful energizing breath of air. That's right...

Unhealthy Role Models

How many young people have thought, "I'm not going to do *that* when I grow up!"? Perhaps they didn't like the way their mother or father spoke or behaved, or maybe they felt sorry for them because they didn't have the self-control a parent should have.

And yet, upon reaching a certain age, that same person might look in the mirror with shock, realizing, "I've become my mother!" I've heard this kind of amazement from many clients, usually accompanied by a lot of frustration because they not only didn't plan on becoming obese – they were determined to be different from unhealthy family members.

I've also met people who blatantly state, "I come from a long line of fat people." It doesn't really matter to me where, when or how that impression was created, it's enough that it exists.

Both of these beliefs, while appearing to be at opposite ends of the spectrum, have something in common: they are usually imprints that are placed upon a child early on in life. Fortunately, they are also malleable and hypnosis is an excellent modality for changing them.

One of my favorite and most effective methods to help people release unhelpful imprints while retaining ones that are desirable is with a cording experience.

Playing with Cords

You don't have to be a new-ager to subscribe to the idea that we are made of energy and we also share and exchange energy with others. A brief discussion with your client might mention how we feel this exchange – some people just make you feel safe and warm while others seem to drain you.

I will offer that when I let myself imagine how that energy is being transmitted, I might visualize some type of cord that flows from my core to another person's core. Via this connection flows a uni-directional energy and I ask the client to close their eyes and get in touch with their own version of it.

Later, after immersing them into a hypnotic state, I will once again draw attention to that energy connection and specifically, to the connection that exists between the client and the source of unhelpful imprints.

Note: Anytime we ask someone to think of something or someone from the past, we are regressing them, so I consider in advance whether I want to dissociate them from the experience and view it from afar or if it's safe for them to be experiencing it in the first person perspective.

With attention on the perceived source of the unhelpful beliefs, I will continue in this vein:

> *As you are there, now...get in touch with the connections you have with this person. Perhaps you can imagine them as strings, ribbons, ties...of all types. Some of them may even be heavy, coarse...like a rope...or even a chain.*

> *These are the things that the two of you share. Some of these things are wonderful and positive...like your love for (describe an interest or a passion the two of them have in common)...while others are not as positive...*

And when you think about...and become fully aware of...the way that you had to learn from this person...a certain way of eating, for instance...like having to eat all of the food on your plate...you can now find the cord, the connection that maintains that habit...see it there...(Get acknowledgment from client)...

And I am now handing you a tool with which you can let go of that habit...that belief...go ahead and sever that attachment...let it go...and let me know when you have done that...

Great...you have now freed yourself from that habit of having to eat all of the food...you can now choose to stop eating before all of the food is gone...and feel good about doing that...

If there are other unhelpful beliefs, imprints or habits, you can continue to identify them individually, then sever them and provide direct suggestion regarding the new responses. After releasing the unwanted cords, it's good to revisit a couple of the positive ones, strengthening them:

Notice that connection between you that represents your love of the outdoors...this person really enjoyed going for walks and you do, too. Let's make that cord even stronger, shall we? I'll give you some special strengthening solution and you can add it to the connection...Let me know when you have done that...

Once the cord work has been completed, suggest that the client let the other party go back to whatever they need to be doing and begin to future pace to cement what you have done. Be sure to compound feelings of empowerment, confidence and self-worth in this experience.

Patter Box

No, thanks...you can take this back. It doesn't belong to me.

Inner Conflict

Many of our clients seek out our help because they are struggling with inner conflict. In the case of people desiring weight loss, there is a part of them that desperately wants to get healthy, changing their relationship with food to change their body and yet there is also a part of them that just wants to play it safe, to stay in a comfort zone even as that gets more and more uncomfortable.

We can use a Parts approach to help people get those differing aspects of their psyche working congruently. There are some excellent trainings on Parts Therapy, or Parts Work as we non-licensed practitioners like to describe it. My colleague here in Washington State, Roy Hunter, for example, is well known for his Parts Work for Inner Resolution. Many of these trainings suggest that you help a client identify the "part", or ego state, that is being problematic; the part of them that is resisting or sabotaging progress.

This is great – we need to know what the problem is in order to fix it. But, I prefer to start with a very positive introduction to the power of Parts Work and to that end, I created a process that does just that. If time allows, I will guide a client through it within a session but if we don't have time for it, I will share an audio of it and request that the client listen on their own. Either approach seems to be effective.

Customize it with any specifics you think will be helpful for your client's needs, too! I wrote it for you to play with it, bend it and develop your own flexibility:

Archetype Alignment Script:

Following initial induction:

> *This hypnosis experience will guide you to a place where you can learn more about yourself...where you can discover inner resources...which will enable you to achieve a greater sense of*

happiness and success in your life... no matter what your specific goals.

Each of us have many different aspects to our personalities ...some of them are more apparent...such as the part of us that is the child of our parent or perhaps the brother or sister to a sibling or maybe even a parent to our child...there is a part of us which yearns at times to be a partner to someone special, in a romantic way or via a more plutonic connection. We may also be aware of the student part of us, or the productive, income-earning part of us or the part of us which loves to engage in sport or physical activities.

These parts exist within us all, to some degree, and they help us navigate through our lives. We may be consciously aware when we are assuming certain identities in a stronger sense, and even when we are subduing others...or, we may have little knowledge of these eternal, internal personalities...

When we are feeling balanced and healthy, the various aspects of our personalities are working in congruence and we find it smooth sailing through life. But when we are struggling, especially with forces in inner conflict, these characters are no longer in alignment.

It is desirable to become aware not only of the many aspects of yourself, but to become aware of how they work for you. This experience is designed to introduce you to some very special parts of your personality, to give you a chance to learn how they influence and help you, and to establish a deeper relationship with them.

It is my objective to be your tour guide here, not to dictate who or what you should be, but to allow you to discover some wonderful innate qualities of yourself which have always been, and will continue to be, within you.

Deepen to a meeting place:

Imagine, now, a meeting place of some type. It might be a large table surrounded by comfortable chairs, it could be an open fire pit with log seating, or perhaps it's a round stone hovering in midair...whatever you prefer is just right for you. Notice that there is a special place for you to sit; it's the place of command and you make yourself comfortable there now.

I'd like you to begin with summoning forth a part of yourself that you are already familiar with; this is the part of you that represents your strength and your ability to take action. We might think of this aspect of yourself as the Warrior, or perhaps you think of it as the Fighter, or the Protector...or even the Hero. You know that this part was present at times in your past when you were feeling a sense of determination, when you were creating the emotional commitment necessary to do whatever you needed to do.

Invite this Inner Warrior to join you in this setting now...and take some time to notice everything about this powerful and focused part of your personality. Notice how your Warrior manifests physically: the shape, the features, any dress or accoutrements, tools or even, weapons.

And now, begin to feel a deep bond beginning to form between you and this formidable champion...let a feeling of trust flow between you as you relay your appreciation and gratitude for all that your Warrior does for you. Your Warrior's ultimate goal is your happiness and success and you can take some time now to reflect on how this part of you plays an important role in your life.

How will you know when your Warrior is working for you, when it is present? Notice the ways...perhaps with a forceful word, a push for action or a firm guiding hand? Let the awareness of how your Warrior works for you imbed itself deep in your mind.

PAUSE

Next, please invite a part of you that is very special. This part of you represents your intuition, your humor, your imagination. It's been described as the Magician, or the Fairy Godmother, or the Maverick...even the Wise Guy!

The ability to tell the silent truth about a situation helps the Magician to find solutions; and this gift often arrives as easily as if by a snap of the fingers or a kiss blown in the air. Your Magician can solve things in an instant, using whimsy and humor...because it's all magic – invisible and ethereal.

Pay close attention as your Magician appears and joins you. This is a part of you which can detach from anything, just sitting to the side, observing it. It may even decide to sit on top of the table, or beneath it! Your Magician is sometimes irreverent, always creative and humorous. Notice how this part manifests physically: the shape, the features, any dress or accoutrements, tools or even, toys.

Take some time now and get to know your Magician... establish a light-hearted connection with this part of your personality that loves to help you through laughter and play and intuition. Your Magician's ultimate goal is your happiness and you can take some time now to reflect on how this part of you plays an important role in your life.

How will you know when your Magician is working for you, when it is present? Notice the ways...perhaps with a quiet chuckle, a flash of insight, a sleight of word? Let the awareness of how your Magician works for you imbed itself deep in your mind.

PAUSE

Now, it's time to invite a wonderful part of you to this gathering. I'd like you to meet the aspect of your personality which signifies your deepest emotional connection to others and to the world itself. This is the part of you which we might call the Lover, or the Loving One. You may also think of it as the Caretaker or the Protector.

The Loving One inside of you is the source of your feeling of connection and compassion for others. The Loving One is the epitome of unconditional love, unconditional acceptance...not just for others, but for yourself. This is the deepest essence of love and is the purest part of who you are.

We are all born with this Loving One and it dwells within us, constantly seeking the opportunity to express the innate, rich and satisfying experience of loving unconditionally. Let your Loving One shine as it joins you here now...see it in all of its glory, all of its brilliance. Notice how this aspect of yourself manifests physically: the shape, the features, any dress or accoutrements, gifts or symbols.

How will you know when your Loving One is working for you, when it is present? Notice the ways...perhaps with a warm hug, a compassionate whisper...a patient smile? Let the awareness of how your Loving One works for you imbed itself deep in your mind.

PAUSE

Please, consider now a part of yourself which can be described as the Sovereign. This aspect resembles a King or a Queen and holds a position of power and ultimate wisdom. Your Sovereign is just and fair and is a source of your personal integrity. As the senior part of this group, it also holds authority over the others and can intercede, dictate and govern on your behalf.

Notice how this aspect of yourself manifests physically: the shape, the features, any dress or accoutrements, gifts or symbols. Spend some time getting to know your King or Queen now...

How will you know when your Sovereign is working for you, when it is present? Notice the ways...perhaps with a wise decision, perhaps with compromise, or maybe by showing you your moral compass? Let the timeless knowledge of how your Sovereign works for you imbed itself deep in your mind.

PAUSE

Will you now, please, turn your attention to the spirit of cooperation between all these aspects of yourself? You might notice how they are balanced or represented to you...Does one of these characters exert more influence than another? Observe how they all work together, or perhaps they haven't been working together very well at all...whatever you notice, I want you to realize that you are in the position of power here; you are the most important one and you are the one in control.

Imagine now that you can adjust anything that needs adjusting, as simply as waving a hand gently in the air and guiding them all toward a balanced point. Maybe you want to adjust the height of the chairs or seats...or blow a kiss to change the light that illuminates each of your parts...

You don't have to think about the details of this; just trust that your dynamic subconscious mind knows how to do this. Take a wonderful, energizing breath...and as you exhale, feel everything fall into place...naturally...perfectly...for you.

Please also observe that these various aspects of your personality enjoy this balancing...and that this draws their attention toward each other, so that they now fully appreciate the value of working together, in congruence for your wishes and desires. See that connection of agreement manifesting now...feel the camaraderie; the love that they share...with you as their common link.

PAUSE

If there is a particular goal that you are desiring in your life...imagine placing that request before you right now...it may be represented by a tangible item, or a word or even just a thought. Just place it out there and ask your personality aspects to help you with this...each one has a way to assist you and will now work independently, yet also as a team to move you toward this goal...this dream...

Thank them; show your gratitude and appreciation for all that they do for you...and when you are ready, let them assimilate back into yourself, where they will now support you in an enhanced endeavor to let you live a happier and healthier life.

Take another, wonderful and deep energizing breath...and as you exhale...let yourself imagine all of the marvelous possibilities that are coming to you as a result of this experience. You will find that from this point forward, you will become more aware of how each aspect of your personality is positively influencing you at certain times...and...you will realize that you can call forth specific ones to help you when you need them...

Following this introduction to Parts Work, your client will be better able to engage in any process that addresses their ego states and especially be able to bring in some of those helpful ones.

I have had many clients refer back to these positive aspects of themselves, and I follow suit, utilizing them in subsequent hypnosis sessions to compound their positive influences. I recall one client who had a professional photograph taken of her in her "Sovereign" ego state, complete with crown and scepter – it was brilliant!

Remember...have fun and good things happen.

Roger Moore, who is a Seattle-based counselor and hypnotist with a long history of helping people in the area of weight loss, created an excellent Parts approach that involves the inner child and I have, over the years, adjusted and augmented it to fit my style. I share it here while acknowledging my good friend Roger's valuable creation and thank him for all that I have learned from him.

Inner Child for Weight Loss (based on a script by Roger Moore)

I am speaking to you about eating and, more specifically, about how you treat and give care to your body. You, as do all individuals, have in your body two opposing forces that struggle for control. One part of you that wants to change and one part that wants to remain the same. One part that wants to reach out and risk and one part that wants to withdraw and play it safe. One part that wants to eat more responsibly and one part that wants to continue eating irresponsibly. For our purposes here today, we are calling these two parts of you the adult and the child.

In the past you have lost contact with that part of you that can control your eating. Perhaps you have felt frustrated, hopeless maybe even defeated. Well, now you are re-awakening that part of you that is full of self-control, drive, and ambition; that part of you that can and will control your eating. First, let's introduce you to these two parts of your personality, the adult and the child. This is important for solving the conflict between these two parts of you. It is essential to healthier living and controlling your weight.

Now, just imagine in your mind that you can see these two parts of your personality standing in front of you right now. These are the two parts of you that are in conflict and are battling for control of your eating. Concentrate and imagine them standing side by side right there in front of you.

Now, take a few moments to introduce yourself to these two parts of your personality. In the front of you and to one side, imagine or feel, in as much detail as you possibly can, the irresponsible, impulsive, overeating part of your personality. This is the part of you that doesn't care about your health. This is the part of you that doesn't care about what you weigh. This is the part of you that doesn't care about how you feel. This is the part of you that is accustomed to your overeating. This is the part of you that is only interested in the instant satisfaction that over eating brings. This is the part of you that always finds a good excuse to abandon your diet. This is the part of you that has sabotaged every attempt you've ever made at controlling your weight. This is the part of you that has been in control of your eating. We can call this irresponsible, impulsive, overeating part of yourself, the child part of your personality.

Standing next to that part, in front of you, and to the other side, feel, picture or imagine, in as much detail as you possibly can, the responsible, caring, protective, loving, nurturing, weight-conscious part of your personality. This is the part of you that cares about your health. This is the part of you that cares deeply about what you weigh. This is the part of you that cares deeply about how you feel. This is the part of you that wants desperately to eat less food, to eat better food, and to give better care to your body. This is the part of you that is tired of the excess weight. This is the part of you that wants to finally gain control of your eating. This is the part of you that decided to use hypnosis to solve your weight issues.

We can call this responsible, protective, weight-conscious part of yourself...the loving, nurturing adult part of your personality. Focus in on these two parts of yourself, the adult and the child. Picture them clearly in your mind. See or feel them both standing there in front of you.

Take a few moments now and notice every little detail about each one of them and be aware of how you feel about both of these characters. Continue to study the adult and the child there in front of you. For they both are very much alive within you and each one has different wants and needs. Each affects you in both positive and negative ways.

Think of your body as being very much like a young child. Just as a young child must accept what its parents choose to feed it, your body has no choice other than to accept whatever you choose to feed it. However, you do have a choice, and you, from this moment on, feel compelled to be a more loving, more nurturing, a more responsible parent for this child. You feel compelled to treat your body with more dignity and more respect. You feel compelled to feed and care for your body more responsibly. For the answer to finally solving this weight control problem for you is right here right now at your fingertips. The answer lies in solving the conflict between these two opposing parts of you.

Once again, study these two characters and notice all of the differences between them. Be aware of how you feel right now about the adult and the child within you. Until now, that child part has largely been in control of your eating. This child has been making the decisions about what and how much you eat. Just as it is inappropriate for a young child to choose its parent's meals, it is also inappropriate for you to allow your inner child to choose your meals for you. This child in you plays a very important role in your world, so we don't want to eliminate this child totally from your life. However, what you eat is a decision that should be made by the responsible, loving, nurturing adult within you and not that impulsive child.

Now, please take that child by the hand...take him/her for a walk, perhaps, or maybe to your favorite place or their favorite place. A safe place, where the two of you can connect for a while. Here, in this place, will you please tell this child how you feel about them? Will you tell them all of the wonderful things you know about this child?

And now, go ahead and have a conversation about eating and food with this child. If fact, will you ask them how they would rather be playing, something else that they'd rather do...instead of making you eat those unhealthy things? Think about the strengths of this child, their interests and abilities...for example, many kids like to be physically active, don't they? They like to run around and move their bodies...maybe walking quickly or dancing. That might be a nice thing for them to do for you. Or, maybe they want to help you be more creative...engaging in some art or music. Or, maybe they just would like to laugh more often...even for no reason! Talk for a while and together, come up with an idea or two...ways that kid can really help you.

And let me know when you've done that.

Good, will you two also figure out a way, a method, a signal of some kind, through which you will know that your inner child is stepping up and helping you? Maybe it will be with a whisper, or a giggle or a little tickle...You get to decide. Let me know when you've done that...Good.

Now, in your mind, turn back to that adult part of you. Just look at that adult part of you and notice that he or she is reaching out to you. Reach out to him or her until you are touching and holding hands with this responsible adult part of yourself. Now, pull your adult part in closer to you and be aware of this strong connection that's beginning to take place between you and the responsible adult within you. As you feel this very powerful force coming alive within you, be aware of how good you are feeling and how confident you are becoming. You form a new bond, a new partnership with this responsible, weight-conscious, caring adult part of your personality.

As I now make some statements to you, imagine that there's a mirror in front of you and that you are looking at yourself in the mirror. As I make these statements repeat them silently to yourself in your head. Repeat them with confidence. Repeat them with certainty. Repeat them with authority. Repeat them with love, and as you repeat these statements to yourself in your head, notice how that image of yourself in that imaginary mirror changes. This image starts out being vague and undefined but transforms into a new image of you that is strong, clear, concise and confident. Allow this change to be felt in both your body and your mind. You can feel yourself becoming this powerful image.

As I now begin making these statements; repeat them after me silently to yourself.

I am now in control of my eating. This control gives me a sense of energy and power like I have never experienced before.

I like myself so much better now that I am in control of my eating.

I feel so much better now that I am in control of my eating.

I am now the loving, nurturing adult giving loving care to my inner child.

These are statements that are motivating you, on a subconscious level. Allow them to be etched into your unconscious mind, your sub-conscious mind.

Concentrate on these statements and this new powerful image of yourself, being aware of how good you are feeling right now as you can feel these changes taking place within you. For you have now directly channeled your own inner ability to control your eating into your sub-conscious mind by putting you in touch with your own responsible, loving inner adult; immediately feeling the benefits as this feeling becomes stronger and stronger leading to more control and more responsible eating.

And with your arms still wrapped around that loving inner adult, now reach out to that little child and together wrap your arms around him or her embracing that child in a hug of unconditional love; unconditional acceptance; allowing all the various parts or aspects of you to now work together in harmony as a winning team supporting you in becoming slimmer, healthier and happier!

Emotional Freedom Techniques for Weight Loss

EFT has gained a lot of attention and acceptance, especially in the field of trauma relief, and certainly merits being incorporated into every hypnosis practitioner's toolkit. I've been using EFT successfully with clients to not only discharge the negative download of life's slings and arrows but as an effective response to unwanted cravings.

One client, who had already reduced over 100 pounds of excess weight through our work together, contacted me in a panic. She begged for an appointment, saying she was afraid she was backsliding with her eating habits.

When we met in a few days, my client told me that she had been having obsessive thoughts about eating Chinese food – thinking about food all day had been one of the ways she had previously felt out of control. Since I had taught my client EFT, I asked her to start tapping on the cravings.

As she did so, I encouraged her to tell her "story" about the cravings – where she felt them, what they felt like, what emotions she noticed as she tapped along the various points on her face. When she got to the meridian point under her nose, she suddenly burst into tears, saying, "I know what it is!"

She then described how she and her best friend used to get together once a week and enjoy talking and laughing over, you guessed it...Chinese food. Since her friend had died a couple of years before in a car accident, not only had my client missed out on the friendship but she had neglected other female relationships in her life.

As she continued to tap into and release some of the grief from losing her friend, it became more and more difficult for her to find the food craving. The process circled around with her knowing now what she needed to do – get in touch with some friends and get together in a healthy way. As soon as she did, you know what happened!

I don't spend an inordinate amount of time using or teaching EFT to my clients. I usually provide them with the Basic Recipe and suggest that this is something they can do privately to promote their own success.

If you haven't used tapping in your practice and are curious, you can check out Gary Craig's website at emofree.com and I also like eftuniverse.com as a place for clients to explore EFT.

Patter Box

> *That was then...and this is now.*
>
> *You know...that it's easy for you to now let go of the weight.*

The Good Girl Syndrome

Even if you aren't familiar with this description, I imagine that you know what it refers to: a tendency to sublimate one's own desires, beliefs and best interests to others in an effort to be accepted and even loved.

I'm no longer surprised that the majority of my weight loss clients have some of these inclinations and that they have been operating under them for most of their lives. When little girls learn, as they do, that they get positive attention when they behave, when they are nice and agreeable, a powerful download of nicety occurs.

One might also wonder if a desire to get along and avoid conflict is biologically wired into women – after all, we aren't historically physically superior to men and it was preferable to keep the peace in order to survive.

Let me also say, in defense of being accused of being sexist, that this mechanism is not limited to the fairer sex. I've worked with some men who have also struggled with how having to be the "nice guy" has influenced their life and their body weight in negative ways. These men relate strongly to the "nice guy finishes last" idea.

So, this type of appeasing program is created and then reinforced throughout the growing up years, causing a person's self-esteem to become wired with compliant behavior. At some point, often in conjunction with puberty, society doesn't respond well to it, providing a growing multitude of unpleasant, painful and otherwise burdensome experiences.

It's not a surprise that people who can't say no to others also have a problem with boundaries over food choices. Helping a client identify and establish personal boundaries when it comes to what they will and what they will not tolerate in life will radiate right into their food choices, besides having a strong influence on growing self-confidence and self-direction...all of which support weight loss.

Once your client has gained awareness that she has difficulty with personal boundaries, you can help her start to create ones that are congruent to her desired authentic life. Some of the processes I use involve shifting perspectives so that insight can be gained while emotional distancing occurs.

Having a client practice having better boundaries is important. A simple exercise involves being able to say "No" to a request that she just doesn't want to do, even if it's coming from a friend or family member. Or, if she describes how she spends all of her money on gifts for others, future pace her with a different and better behavior that will still allow her to show that she cares without draining her financial resources.

A common challenge that weight loss clients encounter is not wanting to hurt people's feelings by turning down food offers. When we help these clients teach others how they want to be treated, we free them from the useless bonds of fear and guilt. They soon discover that, as Dr. Seuss once wrote, "The people who matter don't mind...and the people who mind don't matter!"

Chapter Seven   Changing Preferences

A compelling reason why hypnosis helps in the area of weight loss is the way that it can be applied to actually influence a client's choices when it comes to what they put into their body on a regular basis.

Lack of a sense of control frustrates many clients who come to us for help. It is extremely puzzling to someone who is able to successfully manage many areas of their life, yet be completely helpless in others. We hypnotists understand that the harder one tries, the more resistant entrenched habits can become.

An NLP pattern created by Robert Dilts contains an effective way to help clients gain control through their ability to make better choices. This is how I use the Pragmagraphic Swish:

Begin with helping the client gain further awareness of their unwanted urge or habit by asking them to think of the part of themselves that maintains it. I ask them to close their eyes and think of the different times when this part is activated; times of the day, of the week, of the month, seasonally...times in their life when this behavior is being generated. I tell them they may have flashes of awareness moving through their mind as they do this.

Next, I ask them to recall places, geography, where this behavior has been activated. Places like at home, or out in restaurants, socially, etc.

Finally, I ask them to notice if there are any other people associated with this behavior and, if so, to allow awareness of these people to surface in their mind.

I then ask the client to imagine a recent time or even just a typical time when they might feel the urge or compulsion toward the unwanted behavior. But I ask them to go to the point right before they have the feeling of needing to engage in that behavior, to the time when they realize that they are wanting to. This can also be framed as the moment when they just become aware of the feeling of the habituated impulse or urge.

I ask them to see, hovering right in front of them, between themselves and the behavior, a floating question mark. I ask them how big it is and what color it is. (Many clients find great meaning in the color of their question mark!) You can also focus on other sub-modalities involved with the compulsion at this point.

Next, I ask them to recall how it used to be: they would simply move right through that question mark, straight into that old behavior. This time, though, things are different and I tell them to imagine taking a step (and I encourage them to even do this physically – often teaching this in a standing position) to the right and noticing a vast field of alternate choices. Suggest that they can become aware of a huge selection of things they can select, other than that old, unwanted behavior/choice or even, response.

I ask them to describe some of the alternate choices. You may have to help them with ideas at this point; people who have been operating under the illusion that they are helpless or out of control have rarely spent much time considering how many choices they really have!

As the client is associated into this state of choice and creativity, bring up and anchor any sub-modalities related to this positive resource.

Following this enlightenment, you can move the client back and forth between that "Question Mark Moment" and a position of choice. This "swish-like" action will collapse the old compulsion and create a new automatic response toward positive options.

I usually do this process prior to formal hypnosis, later future pacing the client in hypnosis, adding relevant suggestions to further cement the work. But you can certainly apply the technique while working in an interactive level of hypnosis, too. Case Example:

A client had fallen into the habit of buying a special loaf of bread every time she visited the grocery store. Since she was the only one at home who enjoyed the bread, she found herself unable to avoid eating it when it was in the house. She noted that she never put the bread on her shopping list and didn't even consciously think about it until she was suddenly confronted by it at the end of the aisle, at which point she automatically placed it in her shopping cart.

Following the session in which I taught her this process, the client reported that whenever she was in the grocery store and came into the vicinity, she actually stopped and took a step to the right and smiled as she noticed all of the others things she could select or do, instead of that old, unhelpful grabbing of the bread. She was further able to incorporate the process toward making other, desired choices including how she was emotionally responding to life situations.

Patter Box

> *The question no longer is how do you gain control...but how you choose to take control...as the answer now lies within all of your choices...*

Another novel approach I use to help clients change preferences, whether that if for food choices or other desired behavior is to take a trip down the Parts path. John Cleesattel developed a Parts approach that he calls a "manager's meeting" in which the client is introduced to different aspects of their personality that may play a relevant role in their world. (You can find John's protocols for sale at a very reasonable price at wizardoftrance.com.)

One of these characters, named the "Stubborn Part", is responsible for maintaining the lists of things that the client will do and will not do. Here's how I have taken John's idea and applied it for my clients who want to lose weight:

Imagine now, in whatever way works for you, that part of yourself that is managing your food choices for you. You might think of this aspect of your personality as "The Eater", for example.

Perhaps you want to think about all of the times that this part of you is activated...from the first time that you actually, long ago, began to experience eating food...through all of your childhood, how you learned how to eat and how to enjoy certain foods and how to dislike others...

And maybe you can think now about all of the different places where you ate...and drank. At home, or at someone else's home...out in restaurants...picnics...or at school...Thinking about all those times when that Eater Part of you was helping you...

And if there were others who joined you...or influenced you...think about those now. Maybe they prepared or fed you the food...or maybe they kept you from eating. Just be aware of anyone who was involved in those eating experiences...or beliefs.

And now, I'm talking to that Eater Part of you. I'd like to thank you for all that you have done for _____ and I'd also like to ask you if you would please show _____ the list of foods and drinks that she will eat, along with the list of those she will not. And, _____, you will notice, looking at that list of things that you will eat, perhaps there are some items that have contributed to your weight issues.

(Provide examples, based on client's previous input.)

And look at that list of things that you will not eat. Maybe you notice some things that you have never enjoyed or perhaps you no longer enjoy. I wonder if you ever realized how many things you will not eat...maybe even some things you never even thought about before this moment?

118

...things that are really pretty awful or disgusting...there, on that list.

Now, because you are ready to make some big changes in your eating preferences, I want you to identify something on that list of things that you do eat or drink...something that you are willing to stop eating in order to achieve your goal. Let me know when you have it in mind. (Get details...)

Good. Now, I'm asking that Eater Part of you to move that thing off of the list of things you eat...move it over there, onto the list of things that you do not eat. In fact, if you will put it right between a couple of those disgusting things, that might be good.

Let me know when that has happened.

Great! Doesn't that feel good? Now your conscious mind and your subconscious mind can agree on the things that you will eat and drink and the things you will no longer eat and drink. And the Eater Part of you will enforce this for you, making it even easier to make and maintain the changes that will allow you to release the excess weight.

Note: Get some type of ratification/acceptance from client that the change has happened. Otherwise, some Parts negotiation needs to be implemented prior to re-integrating. Follow with future pacing for success with the specified changes in place.

Reframing Food Preferences

Stanford University recently released results of an interesting study that demonstrate how the description of healthy foods heavily influenced their desirability to diners. Food that was described in "healthy" terms was perceived as being less appetizing, until the exact same food was labeled in a more indulgent manner.

For example, vegetables that were offered as "low-sodium, wholesome, low-cal and nutritious" were consumed at lower levels than the very same vegetables with labels such as "rich, buttery-roasted, sweet, sizzly, tangy, dynamite, etc." The research showed about a 20% difference in participants' eating choices!

Helping a client who is vegetable-adverse is a breeze when we change perceptions in this way. Together, you can identify a few items that they want to add to the "do eat" list and jazz up their presentation!

Sugar and Spice Story for Releasing Sweets Cravings

Stories and poems are wonderful to use with our clients. They entrance both the conscious and subconscious minds and help clients experience profound understanding and shifts in a subtle, yet powerful way. Here is one I wrote for my clients who have unwanted obsessions with sugary things and it's also a good lead in for dealing with clients who have that "good girl syndrome".

> Everyone knows that little girls are made of sugar and spice and everything nice. But, once upon a time, when I was a little girl and spent a lot of time thinking about the weird things that adults said, I wondered what that actually meant...am I really made up of sugar and spice and everything nice?

> I was a rowdy little girl. I behaved more like a tomboy, climbing on stuff, jumping off of rocks, being daring and active and laughing and showing my wit and character to anyone who watched...so I suppose that could be taken to mean that I was spicy...

> But what about the sugar and the nice? That didn't seem to fit me very well and it made me sad that I didn't belong in that phrase about little girls being made of sugar and spice and everything nice.

So I decided to make myself more like sugar. And, being just a little girl with little knowledge of things like health and nutrition, it only made sense to me that in order to be made of sugar, I would need to consume sugar...and so I did...I focused my desire on anything that contained sugar...I spent my waking hours...and my dreaming hours...on the pursuit and consumption of sugar...

At first, this new adventure was really, really fun...I felt like one of the kids in Willy Wonka's Chocolate Factory! I loved getting the taste of sugar in my mouth, and the sticky, sweet remnants on my hands or around my mouth reminded me of how I was becoming "made of sugar"...I searched and found sugar in so many places; I didn't have to look very hard...I realized that sugar was all around me...at home, at school, at my grandmother's house, at school, at my friends' houses, at every store I entered and wrapped around every special holiday...the sugar greeted and invited me to make it part of me!

But, soon, the fun of sugar began to sour. Sometimes I noticed that I didn't feel very well after I ate sugar. While it was in my mouth and going down my throat, I loved the feeling of making it part of me...but once it hit my stomach, that good feeling went away and left me feeling bad inside. And the more I ate sugar, the worse I began to feel. Gradually, I began to realize that the sugar wasn't really good for me, but I still wanted to be a little girl made of sugar and spice and everything nice.

But the rest of that saying, the "everything nice", meant that I had to keep these bad feelings to myself. When a little girl is nice, it means that she goes along with everyone and is sweet (because of the sugar) and is obedient because she is nice. Maybe I knew that I should be nice to the sugar, too, even though it had started to make me feel bad.

And this went on for a very long time. And even though I knew the sugar was not really nice to me, I kept it close to me, even when it started to contribute to my health in so many ways, like making me overweight, or ruining my teeth or complexion, or even giving me illnesses. I just wasn't ready to give up being made of sugar and spice and everything nice.

But then, one day, as I was sitting down to eat a big piece of my favorite, sugary snack, I heard a little, tiny voice inside my head...it was an itty-bitty squeak of a voice...one I hadn't heard in a long, long time, since I was a little person...and that voice said, "Stop." And I started to sob...but I wasn't crying tears of sadness, I was crying tears of joy. I finally heard that little girl inside me and I was so happy to talk with her again.

And we sat together, she and I, and we talked about the truth about little girls and what they are really made of and she helped me let go of the lies and she helped me embrace the truths...and when we were done, we hugged and I held her tight, never to let her go again...and I picked up that sugary snack and I walked over to the trash bin and I threw it away.

And I never, ever again believed that stupid saying about what little girls are made of. Now I know what I am made of and it's healthy and strong and it speaks out, even when it's not nice.

Aversion Therapy

Years ago, I attended a workshop offered by someone who was well known as a successful weight loss hypnotist. As somewhat of a newbie, I was looking for specific ideas on how I could better assist my own weight loss clients. One of my adult daughters accompanied me and we sat next to each other in the filled-to-capacity room.

Somewhere during the talk, the presenter announced that she would now guide us through some visual imagery and asked us to imagine a food that was troublesome to our good health – something that we would prefer that we not put into our body.

I imagined some corn chips, as I had an affinity for that salty, crunchy snack, despite it not being a healthy choice. As we were guided into visualizing the food item, this hypnotist told us that we were bringing it up, closer and closer, toward our mouth...until suddenly we saw that it was covered with something really disgusting. Now, she didn't specify what that something was, because we all knew on some level how to fill in the blank.

Upon hearing this suggestion, I immediately opened my eyes and dropped my hand. I noticed that my daughter had also done this, along with several other people in the room. Rapport, for me, was destroyed and I listened to the rest of the lecture with a bit of dismay. I was happy, though, to go away with one important lesson: when using aversion therapy, it is vital to gain permission from your client.

I have since learned that not only is it crucial to gain permission, but you need to offer it in a way that a client doesn't feel pressured or obligated to engage in aversion tactics. After all, as their hypnotist you are their perceived authority on what will work to help them. If you are like me and you prefer to work in a client-centered manner, you want to empower your client with their own authority, so that means using discretion and judgment about who might be a candidate for aversion therapy and how you might use it.

Some guidelines for effective and respectful aversion therapy that I find helpful include:

- Use your client's preferred perception modality for best results. Employing visual imagery for someone who doesn't visualize well won't be effective.
- Offer it as an idea that sometimes helps, but isn't for everyone.
- Be sure to ask the client to provide the descriptions.
- Ask specifically what they want to address and to what extent.

- Pay careful attention when applying aversion and respond to strong reactions, if necessary. You don't want to have to deal with a client vomiting in your hypno-chair!

So, while aversion approaches are not my initial intervention of choice, I have had clients request them. One client, for example, who was diabetic and needed some serious sugar intervention, described how, in the breakroom at work, there was a never-ending supply of donuts. Since she had to walk through this room to get from one area to another, she often would grab a donut and eat it on the run.

My client told me that she really didn't want to be eating any donuts at all and asked for me to "make them unappealing". I then asked her to describe something that was unappealing to her, something that she would never want to eat, much less have near her face. She immediately suggested "anal gland secretions" (she happened to work in the veterinarian field and had up-close history with that disgusting substance).

I easily moved her into a light trance state where I guided her toward those donuts, engaging all of her senses in anticipation of eating one as she raised her hand in response to my suggestions. When I described the donut as having that anal gland material leaking out of the center, she shuddered and dropped the imaginary donut, making a terrible expression of disgust.

Following this experience, my client was very happy and sure that she would not succumb to the allure of the donuts. In fact, she did not and continued to refer to donuts as "dog-nuts" whenever she boasted about her ability to resist them!

Another positive experience with aversion therapy came when a client I had been working with for several months was finally ready to dump her 50 year-long affair with Pepsi. Although we had been able to make many helpful adjustments that were resulting in significant weight loss, she had been clinging to that soda habit.

With her request in mind to be completely free from drinking that beverage, I brought her, in hypnosis, to a table that was filled with a variety of different containers of Pepsi – from individual cups, to cans and bottles of all sizes, the table was overflowing with offerings of her favorite drink. I then began to suggest that she start to drink the Pepsi...noticing how wonderful it tastes, the fizzy effect that she loved, the sweetness, etc.

I continued to have her drink from that table selection, more and more...noticing how the flavors were changing a bit...that the fizziness was becoming flat...that she was becoming full. In fact, after a while, she noticed that her body was starting to swell...her shoes becoming tight, her fingers puffing...and yet, she continued to drink...all of that Pepsi...almost like it was all of the Pepsi that she had put in her body over those 50 years...growing bigger and bigger...uncomfortably big...

It soon became apparent that my client was quite uncomfortable and resisting drinking any more, at which point I whisked the table away and moved her into a healing place, a place where her body could be not only restored, but could begin a healing process and recover from that Pepsi onslaught.

This experience left my client with quite a taste in her mouth about Pepsi, one that would keep her from imbibing it from that point on. Oh, she shared that she just had to test and see, so about a week later, she took a sip and found that it tasted awful to her. While I had not given any suggestions specifically about that, it was obvious that her subconscious had experienced the hypnotic Pepsi as detrimental and was protecting her from putting any more of the real "Devil's Urine" into her body. And without that harmful drink, my client found even more success and continued to release unwanted excess weight.

Chapter Eight   Mind-Body Practices

People who experience illness, accidents and other trauma to the body often react by dissociating from painful sensations and awareness of physical self. While this may be useful in the short term, it can also interfere with a person's ability to self-regulate and make positive changes in behavior.

Obesity is a form of trauma in itself and weight loss clients often are disconnected from their bodies – this is one reason why they can overeat and not be aware of the signals of physical satiation. When it comes to habits and behavior that may not be helpful to a client's improvement or wellness in general, parts of the body may be participating negatively, despite the person's conscious desire to do otherwise.

Our goal is to not only educate clients about their own mind-body communication, which happens to be bi-directional, but to help them become more adept in using it as a healing tool. Because of this two-way function, we can take a "top down" approach, changing the way a person thinks and feels to affect changes in their physiology or, we can take a "bottom up" tact by changing physical functions to improve a person's thoughts and emotional states.

One way I help clients move toward improving how they listen and attend to their body's messages, along with creating self-acceptance, is to use a belly meditation. This approach can also help resolve digestive issues that have been promoted by toxic eating and drinking or even, stressful states.

The belly is really a source of energy, a powerhouse in itself. The Japanese refer to this center of our body as "hara", a place where "ki", or energy, is generated. I learned to embrace and focus on this part of my body during my martial arts training and once I did, I broke through some previous mental and physical limitations.

Releasing unhelpful tension in the belly will calm the entire body and mind, resulting in multiple positive effects:

1) Reduces chronic stress, anxiety and relieves the suffering of pain

2) Improves digestion and stimulates the "digestive fires"

3) Builds self-acceptance

4) Strengthens mind-body communication and enhances an awareness of physical sensations

Mindful Hypnosis Belly Meditation

In some cultures, ours included, people are admonished at a young age to "Suck in your belly!" (Are you unconsciously holding tension in yours right now?!) We grow up with a sense of self-consciousness and even shame about this area of our body, regardless of our size or weight. As a result, we often are disconnected from our belly and may hold negative thoughts about it.

Even if a person doesn't struggle with being overweight, they may be unconsciously "holding" the gut in entrenched and restricted function. Practicing this Belly Meditation can help the enteric nervous system - the digestive tract - move into a more comfortable "remembered wellness".

Sit quietly, with eyes closed. Bring your thoughts to your mid-section, your belly. Become aware of how you feel about this part of your body. Let the thoughts, ideas, judgments flow upward into your awareness, like bubbles floating up from the depths. Do not be your thoughts, just pay attention to them. You may notice that you hear your own voice or you may also hear these thoughts in someone else's voice. Just pay attention to them as they float up.

Next, begin to breathe in a rhythmic way...you can count your breath as you breathe in, count as you hold your breath, and count as you breathe out. You want to breathe deeply, using

128

the diaphragm, so that your belly inflates rather than your chest area. This is an easy way to help your conscious mind step away from distracting or intrusive thoughts and to trigger the Relaxation Response. You may choose to add some imagery to it, such as seeing a number written in sand, then watching a gentle wave wash it away, replacing it with the next number. Or, you may just decide to simply think the numbers in your mind.

As you do this, notice that your stomach muscles are relaxing and as it does, other muscles in your body relax. It is only when your stomach relaxes that it becomes possible for all tension in your body to dissipate...fade away. Soon you become very comfortable, a wave of comfort moves through you and allows your mind to become calm...peaceful.

Now, move your right hand to the top of your abdomen, resting it loosely just below your bra line. Pressing gently, begin to rotate it to the left, in a clockwise direction. You will softly massage the outer circumference of your belly...moving out to the edges of your ribs, dropping down to below the navel and then circling back up the other side. A gentle pressure will move your skin and flesh but will not feel uncomfortable.

Imagine, as you massage your "hara", that you are activating and balancing the life force within you. You are connecting with this intimate, powerful center within. If you find that negative thoughts or feelings are present, let them float up and out. Imagine anything that is blocking, limiting, or otherwise destructive to you is being dislodged and discharged.

Continue to breathe comfortably and rhythmically, inhaling wonderful, healing properties and exhaling anything that is not helpful or healing. Imagine your amazing digestive system functioning perfectly, restored to ideal health.

129

Welcome in a sense of calm...a sense of well-being...even as you feel the energy within your belly become revitalized and renewed.

Once you have completed 10-12 massage rotations, stop and now linger in the feelings of comfort and peace, knowing that when you return to your normal activities, you will feel the positive effects of taking this special time.

Spend several minutes a day in Belly Meditation and within a short period of time you will find that you not only feel differently about your belly and your body as a whole, you will notice improvement in your digestive function!

Note: If you haven't already done a belly mediation, give yourself a little break from reading this book and do it now! You will thank me!

Body Parts

We can also use a "Body Parts" approach to enhance mind-body communication. This approach can be a stand-alone technique or it can easily augment other tools that you use to help a client. In fact, it serves as an excellent process for induction and deepening a client for further work. It helps to create expectation that you are going to "open the dialogue" between a client's conscious and subconscious mind, allowing them to speak directly to parts of themselves that will be part of a healing "team".

Begin by inducing some focus and relaxation in the client. You can have them focus on breath; they can fixate their vision on a hand or leg...guiding them to closing their eyes and noticing that they can still visualize that part of their body, even with eyes closed. The main goal is to direct their attention to their physical self.

From here, use something similar to the following:

As you are aware of your hand, there, now...you can think about all of the things that hand does for you...how it helps you in so many ways...touching, stroking, gripping, grasping, lifting, folding, feeding...(describe any tasks that are relevant to the client)

...what a wonderful hand that hand is...I wonder if you can tell it what you think of all that it does for you?

PAUSE

And, if that hand could speak, what would it say to you? About what it needs from you?

PAUSE

That's right...and now please think about your heart...that amazing pump that causes blood to circulate...keeping you alive. Your wonderful heart that are designed to beat so many times in your lifetime. Now, no one knows exactly how many times that is...but it is working to fulfill that number of beats for you. What do you want to tell that heart?

PAUSE

And, what does that heart want to say to you...about what it is going through...about what it needs from you? Listen to it now...

PAUSE

*That's right...and now please think about your big toe on your left foot (*or some other, unaffected part of the body, maybe an eyebrow or an ear...)...that lovely big toe that helps you stay balanced...helping you walk. Your wonderful big toe is designed to help you take many steps in your lifetime.*

Now, no one knows exactly how many steps that is...but it is working to fulfill that number of steps for you. I wonder if you can let yourself be filled with appreciation of how well that toe is working for you...and will continue to do so.

PAUSE

And would that toe now like to talk to (any body part that needs healing)? Let that happen...what would they say to each other?

PAUSE

Can you imagine...pretend if you have to...that all of that wellness in that toe can be transferred in some way...perhaps even the code for that wellness can be copied and pasted somewhere else in your body...anywhere that it is needed...now...(provide patter that describes where and how

That's right...and now please think about your lungs...those beautiful lungs that take in and process fresh air for you...keeping you alive. Your wonderful lungs that are designed to breathe in and out so many times in your lifetime. Now, no one knows exactly how many times that is...but they are working to fulfill that number of breaths for you. What do you want to tell those lungs?

PAUSE

And, what do those lungs want to say to you...about what they are going through...about what they need from you?

I might suggest that a client have a serious talk with their knees...their liver...any part of the body that has been suffering from lifestyle choices. I can also have the client elicit the help of their hands, which are always complicit in unhealthy eating behaviors, so that they may work more congruently with the client's goals.

132

Following these conversations, suggest that ALL parts of the body integrate together, as part of the whole...working together toward wellness, promoting comfort, balance, healing, continued enlightenment and improvement, etc.

*We can bring in a healthy body part with a couple of strategies:

1. As a pattern interrupt from dealing with the serious side of being overweight or obese, briefly moving attention away from what is wrong toward what is right with the body.

2. As a resource for the parts of the body needing healing.

Any part of the body that is being affected adversely by excess weight can be addressed in this way. Making a space for an intimate dialogue between a client and their body can provide them with awareness, insights and motivation, along with encouraging healing responses in the body.

Additionally, some clients who are struggling with health issues reveal that they feel either let down by their body or that they have somehow let their body down. Encourage the client to maintain a positive and supportive conversation with the body parts they have "talked to"; having a better relationship can help to ease these feelings.

Utilize what your client has revealed about how they feel about their body and help them create a dynamic and ongoing conversation with body parts as an interesting and productive part of your work.

Body Image

Perhaps you have already experienced clients who come in and say, "I saw myself in a photograph and I didn't recognize myself!" Why is it that we can change slowly over time, without conscious awareness of what is happening? Perhaps it's a protective aspect of our mind, maybe it's a form of denial...The truth is that at some point, a person's attention finally locks onto what has happened and it can be shocking for them to "wake up" to reality.

If you have ever watched an episode of "My 600lb Life", the television show in which extremely obese people turn their lives around with weight loss surgery and other means, you will see this happen, over and over again. The profiled person "suddenly" finds themselves morbidly obese and can't believe that they got into that state. This perception distortion becomes even more problematic when they lose weight and still see themselves as being obese. I recall one episode where a woman who, following a surgery for excess skin removal, failed to heal well because she was walking as if she still weighed 700lbs, swinging her now slim hips around furniture and through doorways. Her mind had not caught up to where her body now was!

Another way that body dysmorphia appears is with clients who believe they are fat when they clearly are not. In worrisome cases, this condition can lead to bulimia, anorexia and other dangerous eating disorders. It's important that you pay attention to any appearance of such impressions and refer out to mental health professionals if you are not one yourself.

I had a particularly insightful moment one year when my then-high school-aged son attended a presentation at school. He came home looking strange. I asked him what was going on and he burst forth, enthusiastically talking about the speaker, a woman whose teen daughter had perished from anorexia.

The thing that had really gotten to him, beyond the loss of a fellow young person from a seemingly self-inflicted disease, was some of the language the woman described. She had explained how, in the absence of understanding and ability to describe emotions, young people and even grown adults often just say, "I feel fat."

The word, "fat", can substitute for all of the emotions a person was really feeling, whether it was really feeling lonely, depressed, frustrated, exhausted, etc. "Fat" encapsulates feelings in more way than one, whether a person is applying that word to themselves...or to others.

It's not hard to understand why a client may not see their actual selves in a mirror or even in a hypnotic experience of dissociation. They have most likely been pretty good at creating negative hallucinations until they've started their healing journey with you. Creating a shield of denial regarding what they are seeing and feeling has helped them get up out of bed and function, albeit uncomfortably, every day.

Because of this, it's not uncommon for things to get a little more uncomfortable before improvements arrive. While I don't suggest this to a beginning weight loss client, if they find that they aren't immediately responding to hypnosis or even moving backwards, I reassure them that it's not unusual to have a bit of rain before the sunshine and ask them to trust the process.

My goal is to wake up my client, to all of what's been happening in and around them, so that they can start to get a handle on things. This means that they need to see themselves realistically and that they may need to experience some of the things they've been avoiding.

As they start to do this, with gentle and supporting guidance, things begin to discharge and shift toward wellness. It usually only takes an experience or two to get the ball rolling in the right direction but our belief that it will happen is a big part of success, so keep your eyes on the big picture and don't get distracted by minor setbacks.

Patter Box

> *More and more, you are beginning to see your true self while more and more of the unwanted weight departs...and this fills you with a feeling of lightness and joy...that supports all of the positive changes you are experiencing!*

Virtual Gastric Band

About a decade ago, I started hearing the buzz about a hypnotic version of a weight loss procedure that used a gastric band, also known as a lap band, to restrict the amount of food that a person could consume in a sitting. Apparently, a couple of hypnotists from England were vacationing in Spain and noticed that lots of Europeans were receiving these surgical interventions, hoping to drop excess weight. They wondered, "Could an imaginary, hypnotic version work as well?" And so the virtual gastric band idea was hatched.

I conducted some research and decided to offer my clients the HypnoBand, created by John Maclean, signing on for a license, which at the time were granted on a territory basis in order not to over-flood the market. John's fee was quite reasonable and he didn't even want any continuing piece of my HypnoBand pie, which sure impressed me. Included in my package were guidelines, scripts and audios that contained most everything I needed to guide a client through the process.

Points I like about a Virtual Gastric Band approach:

- Great hook – it really captures a potential client's attention and imagination. I found that it brought clients to me that probably would never have thought of using hypnosis for weight loss.
- It appeals to those who appreciate medical and anatomical references. Nurses, in particular, have been very responsive, perhaps in part because they have actually seen in person the negative effects of weight loss surgery.
- For clients who find "therapy" stigmatizing, coming in for a mental procedure seems to be more acceptable. Often, once I got them in my clutches, the walls came down and we could really get to the crux of their weight problems.
- Despite the clinical nature, it really is a fun process and you know me and fun!

Points I do not like about a Virtual Gastric Band approach:

- Clients are more likely to believe that it's a simple, magic pill and that they don't have to put much effort into the whole project.
- It's not a stand-alone tool. In order for permanent shifts to occur, the relationship to not just food but to their own emotions and bodies needs to be adjusted.
- It's difficult to judge whether suggestions have stuck or a client is mainly just being compliant. I don't really care, personally, as long as they experience success.
- Clients who have had negative medical experiences have a higher potential for freaking out and flexibility is necessary. Hypnotists with less experience may be intimidated.

There are several competent trainers who will teach you how to provide a virtual gastric band service to your weight loss clients. Any such program, in my opinion, should also include many of the things you are learning in this book!

Patter Box

> *My body is my temple and I worship it, by bringing it only the best, most nutritious food, only when it is hungry.*
> ~ Vivienne Filiatreault

Chapter Nine   Managing Symptoms

The Relaxation Response

If there was just one, single reason for using a hypnotic approach to help people lose weight, that would be the benefit it brings by relaxing mind and body. Moving overweight people out of chronically over-stressed states should be a primary goal. When we help a client activate a relaxation response, moving the ANS (autonomic nervous system) from a sympathetic to a parasympathetic state, a healing environment becomes available automatically.

To do this, we can take advantage of what nature has built into us, a rhythmic cycle of activity and rest, to promote healing. Many people are familiar with the Circadian Cycle, which regulates our sleep patterns, but another, interesting rhythm within us is the Ultradian Rhythm.

In our modern, high-paced culture productivity is of great value. When we need to take a break, signals such as loss of focus, hunger, thirst or restlessness are often ignored and instead, people reach out for quick ways to stay on point, including caffeine and unhealthy foods. The body then begins to draw on stress hormones to help, which sustains being in sympathetic nervous system arousal. In turn, this response wears on the natural capacity to self-regulate body functions and emotional states. In the fight or flight response, one is less able to think objectively and begins to react, rather than respond to life.

And, even worse, due to the conditioned wiring of such states, when people don't have to be working, they fail to allow themselves to really relax! This is a major influence of chronic insomnia, which plagues about 10% of Americans.

To operate at our best, it is necessary to take a break about every 90 minutes or so. The conscious mind will actually do this, often below our awareness. Think of times when you noticed that you had "spaced out" or caught yourself daydreaming.

Ernest Rossi has conducted a lot of research on this topic and he coined the phrase, "The Ultradian Healing Response". He prescribed a 20-minute break every ninety minutes or so to recharge the mind and body. For people whose lives are just too busy to afford a 20-minute break, inserting brief recesses periodically during the day can achieve similar positive results.

I teach my clients to utilize Mindful Hypnosis, a term I coined that utilizes interactive hypnotic states, to restore their mind-body and, more importantly, stay ahead of chronic tension and stress. I suggest they call it a "recess" and ask them when they think would be good times to fit it into their schedule. My recipe:

1) Teach them rhythmic breathing.

2) Have them count on the intake, as they hold the breath and again on the exhale of their breath.

3) Time them for a minute, calibrating how they feel before and after.

4) Use this same process to begin induction to formal hypnosis.

There are many recipes for breathing and I offer choices to my clients:

- 5-4-5 Pattern (Breathe in for 5, hold for 4, exhale for 5)
- 7-11 Pattern (Breathe in for 7, exhale for 11)
- Square Pattern (Breathe in for 5, hold for 5, exhale for 5, pause for 5)

Note: I teach most clients (those who can do so easily) to breathe through the nose, not the mouth. Mouth breathing has been associated with decreased levels of blood oxygen and increased levels of anxiety, among other negative effects.

Release Mental Tensions

Many people find it difficult to calm their busy minds, having been conditioned by decades of multi-tasking, worrying and caring for others. This Mindful Hypnosis process will help them quiet that "popcorn on the mind", promoting the relaxation response and enhancing quality of sleep.

Something that I often add to an initial hypnosis experience, wherein we are laying down the foundation for our work and tapping into internal resources, is to encourage the client to let go of anything that is keeping them from feeling at peace. I suggest that they discover a container, a receptacle of some type, into which they can deposit those things without having to actually do an inventory of them.

Providing a place of safe-keeping for worries, doubts, fears and anything else that may limit a sense of peace and comfort paves the way for embracing thoughts and feelings that support good health and happiness.

As those limitations are being stored, I explain that not only will they be safe, but that the client can always go back and get them, if they need to, or that we may deal with them, or, that they may decide to just leave them there.

Whatever imagery or experience is created by this can be anchored and drawn upon at subsequent sessions or even in a client's daily life. The goal is not to ignore responsibilities or vital demands but to empower a person to be able to selectively filter and release anything that is not serving them when it comes to achieving their goals.

Note: I have included a script for this process in the appendix at the end of this book: *Take a Trip to Your Perfect Place.*

Sound Sleep Formula

Quality of sleep experience is linked to many of our clients' presenting problems, including chronic stress, fatigue, focus and memory challenges, weight and chronic pain levels. Helping a client establish and maintain proper sleep hygiene can make all the difference in their success for specific goals.

Begin with assessing your clients' sleep hygiene habits – here is a list of tips from my friend and a great hypnotist, Kevin Cole:

1. Your body likes routine, so aim to go to bed at the same time nightly. Begin winding down about an hour before you go to bed.

2. Avoid caffeine, especially from late afternoon onwards, as it has a stimulating effect for up to 6 hours.

3. Avoid using alcohol to sleep - it produces a shallow, unrestful quality of sleep.

4. Decide bed is for nothing other than sleeping (and making love) - so avoid eating, watching television, telephoning, knitting, having serious discussions, etc.

5. Keep clocks out of sight! Many people create a mini-neurosis through lying awake and checking the clock every few minutes to calculate how much sleep they are missing!

6. Never stay awake in bed for more than about 30 minutes. Have a list of boring/unpleasant tasks beside your bed. Get up and do something from this list if necessary. The idea here is to break the association between being in bed and experiencing insomnia.

7. Avoid rewarding middle-of-the-night waking with food, drink, cigarettes, etc.

8. Avoid day-time naps. Sleep requirements vary so if you don't need a lot of sleep why not use the time constructively - study, hobby, voluntary work, etc.

Many people find that merely participating in hypnosis sessions and/or listening to a relaxing hypnosis recording results in improved sleep. It is believed that by doing so, the brain becomes entrained to be able to let go easier, allowing one to fall asleep easier and stay asleep for longer, uninterrupted periods.

My personal theory, which has absolutely no scientific substance to support it, whatsoever, is that another reason for the sleep experience improvement is that the subconscious mind, which is in charge of our sleep, automatically shifts once a person has decided to use hypnosis to address an issue. It's almost like that part of the mind says, "Finally! Now I don't have to keep bothering her/him at night!"

Here is a basic formula that works for most clients:

1) Create expectation in the client that hypnosis will help them improve sleep (use the ideas presented above and/or offer examples of other people who have found success through hypnosis.)

2) Provide hypnotic experience that contains:

    a. Progressive Muscle Relaxation or Autogenic Training that includes mindful attention to the physical changes

    b. Putting aside mental tensions and distractions (described previously)

    c. Anchoring of best relaxed state with instruction to be able to access it again

3) Future Pacing that gives the client the choice of using one or all of the above methods. Anchor placing the head upon the pillow as a cue to begin to let go of awake and embrace sleep.

4) Provide a recording to support sound sleep. I include the script for my popular *Float to Sleep* mp3 in the Appendix.

Depending on the client's needs, hypnotherapy may be needed to resolve issues that are influencing sleep - including entrained hyper-vigilance, snoring of mate, chronic pain, any unhealthy eating/drinking habits, etc.

Note: Clients who have developed a dependency on medications such as Ambien, or even over-the-counter sleep aids, should be advised to use caution regarding an abrupt cessation of their usage. In these cases, hypnotic approaches may not be immediately successful due to the dependency. A gradual weaning off the drugs while practicing hypnosis will result in success over a period of time.

Patter Box

> *Simply by resting your head upon your pillow, your mind and your body recognize that it is time to begin to let go of awake and embrace sleep...*

Laughter Therapy for Weight Loss

In our book, "Laughter for the Health of It", Dave Berman and I talk about what happens when a person laughs for no reason other than the fact that it's good for you. Just like with hypnosis, the body responds positively to laughing regardless of whether it is based on humor or not.

Some of the helpful things that happen when you practice laughter therapy, which is based on simple and fun laughing exercises, include:

- the release of unnecessary stress and tension
- a reduction in suffering from pain
- production of feel-good neurochemicals like dopamine and serotonin
- automatic pattern interrupts and reframing from negative thoughts and experiences

And specifically, giving your internal organs a workout is a good thing when it comes to releasing excess weight...

The secret of using laughter therapy lies in doing it often and not having it be dependent on jokes. Just like with hypnosis, there is a part of the mind-body that doesn't know the difference between reality and fantasy, so by just practicing laughter, a positive response is created and regular laughter therapy entrains it even more.

One laughter exercise I teach weight loss clients is to laugh out loud at the scale or laugh at the refrigerator – particularly when either of those two are being problematic. People often report back to me that this simple intervention not only lightens their mood but relieves them of the desire to eat for comfort or distraction.

Another useful laughter exercise is what I dubbed, "Laugh-n-Tap", combining EFT tapping with laughing out loud. Clients find they can tap and laugh food cravings, stressful feelings, and even chronic pain away in just a few seconds.

One client who had a daily habit of drinking high-calorie espresso beverages started laughing aloud as she passed the local Starbucks business. It wasn't long until she felt a great victory as she cruised past that location with a big grin, feeling free and becoming healthier every day.

Patter Box

> *The heart can be light and filled with laughter. Life can be taken in stride and spontaneous smiles can burst forth in a flash. The sense of humor can be developed fully, finding lightness in every situation. It is possible to be absolutely free to be oneself...to be light and free.*
>
> ~Sherry Hood

Control Room for Comfort

This classic approach is instructional in nature, providing the client with the experience of learning how metaphorical thoughts and imagery can shift perceptions and even physiological responses. Following is an example of how it may be used for inducing physical comfort, but you can imagine how it can be applied for just about any physical or emotional component.

This is an interactive technique, so a light state of trance is all that is needed to suspend disbelief and entice the client's imagination. Following induction:

Introduce the idea of a "control room" of sorts, within the client's safe/perfect place. You can use some imagery such as a gateway, doorway, etc., depending on your preferences. Guide the client into this space. I use patter such as, "notice that this room is vast...unlimited, limited only by your imagination, which is limited..."

Sample script:

> Notice that the walls of this space are lined with banks of softly flashing, colored lights...instrument panels...dials, levers, gauges of types...I want to tell you that this control room monitors and regulates everything in and about you.
>
> One area measures, calibrates and adjusts all of your physical functions...everything about your body is controlled in this area. Another area is in charge of your emotions, your feelings. Still another section of this Control Room addresses your beliefs, your hopes and dreams.
>
> I'd like you to focus on that area that controls your physical body...your anatomy...In fact, please focus in on the controls for your left hand...

Allow some time here

Let me know when you have found the controls for your left hand...

Good. Now, you will notice that there are many ways that your left hand can be and feel. You might see some controls for the strength or the weakness of your left hand...you might see some controls for the tension or the relaxation of your left hand...perhaps there is an itch adjustment for your left hand...You will also notice that there is a temperature gauge for your left hand. Look and see what the setting is right now. It may appear to you as a digital read-out or it may be in some color spectrum or identified by specific words. The control mechanism may be a dial, or a gauge or a lever...Just notice the temperature of your left hand...right now. Let me know when you are aware of this.

Good. Now, what I'd like you to do is turn down the temperature of your left hand. I want you to turn it way down. Just adjust that temperature control down. I want you to turn it down so far that you soon notice a sense of cooling coming in. You may notice it first on the top of your hand, or perhaps in the fingertips or maybe in the palms. Just notice as your left hand starts to cool. Really turn that temperature down...so that in a little while, a sense of numbness begins to arrive. A sensation of no sensation...numb, like when you have your gums numbed at the dentist. Or, if you like, the feeling you might get if you put your entire hand into a snowbank...or a bucket of ice water. So cold, so numb...now. Some people even notice that it starts to feel as if there is no hand...or, that it feels like a block of wood...inanimate...totally numb. Let me know when your left hand is so numb, it almost feels like it's not there...

Allow enough time for this to occur.

Great! Isn't it interesting how adept you already are at controlling your body sensations? Why, it only took a short

147

while for you to bring all of that numbness into your hand! Wouldn't it be helpful if you could do that anytime you wanted to? In fact, wouldn't it be wonderful if you could then transfer that feeling to any other part of your body...some part where you wanted to have some numb feeling, some relief?

Of course, it would...and you may not be surprised to know that you wouldn't even necessarily have to move that numb hand to that body part...that you can just think of it transferring that numb, sensation of no sensation to that area and very quickly gain that numbing relief. OR, you might decide to just go straight to the controls for that body part and let the relief come right in...that might even be the way you decide to go...

You can now help the client address certain areas of discomfort, while also giving the caveat that this approach should not be used in lieu of medical attention when needed.

You really have to hand it to your mind...because your mind knows how to make you feel better when you decide you are ready and now you are ready to start to warm up that left hand...So, just turn that temperature back up...move it back up to the original degree...notice how the feeling comes drifting quickly back in...so that you are becoming, once again, aware of the feelings of your fingers, your thumbs, the palms...and the backs of your hands. Nice.

Of course, it might be fun to see what it feels like to warm your left hand even more...turning that temperature up even more now...really crank it up...let your begin to get hot...feel that warmth, that heat flowing into your hand...completely...You may even notice the outside air feels like it's chilled...Perhaps you imagine warming your hand next to a crackling bonfire or submerging it in a hot, sudsy bath...Very warm...even hot...now...Maybe there is even a bit of perspiration forming between your fingers or on your palm...So hot...Let me know when your left hand is very warm and even hot...

Excellent! You are so good at this. When you are ready, you can turn back down the temperature of your left hand...let it return to the perfect level for you. You now understand that you can adjust how your left hand and how any part of your physical self is feeling, simply by coming to this Control Room and accessing the controls. You will even notice that you are not limited to just one modality for your body. For example, you can certainly turn down the discomfort and turn up the comfort...or you can turn down tension and turn up relaxation...can't you?

You are the one who knows your body best...you may decide to choose a numb feeling or you may realize that a feeling of warm relaxation is more helpful. But what you have certainly learned here is that you are the Boss of You. You can choose how you feel, at any time...and the more you practice and play here in this Control Room, the easier it becomes for you to elicit the feelings you want.

In fact, wouldn't it be interesting to see how you can adjust things like...your appetite...or your energy levels...or some of your moods?

Pause and let that sink in...

I wonder if you even know how easy it will soon be for you to simply imagine the controls and quickly adjust them..as you begin to gain control through exercising your power of choice...

.and this helps make your life experience even more comfortable, more joyful...after all, that's what you desire and you deserve it! Everyone deserves to live in comfort and joy...

Speaking of gaining control, consider turning your clients who suffer from chronic pain to the HOPE Coaching Comfort Scale. I created this along with Michael Ellner and Alan Barsky; we find many clients prefer measuring their state of being with this frame:

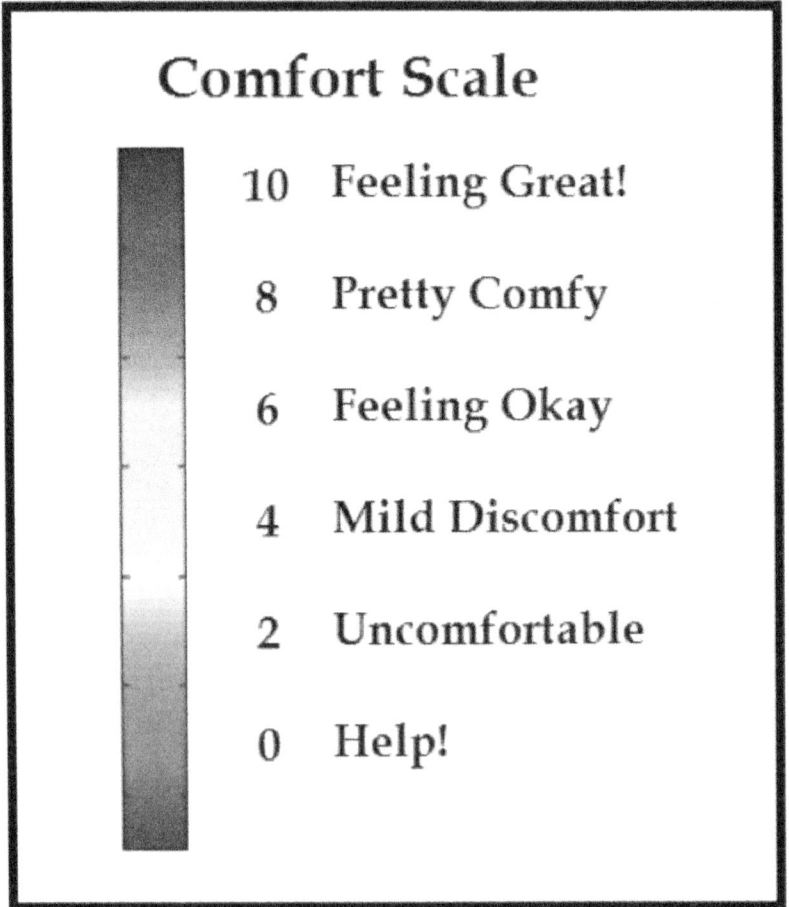

Comfort Scale

10 Feeling Great!

8 Pretty Comfy

6 Feeling Okay

4 Mild Discomfort

2 Uncomfortable

0 Help!

Autogenic Training

For over a decade now, one of my favorite go-to approaches for clients is an autogenic (from within) training exercise, which is effective for a couple of reasons:

- Activates a relaxation response
- Teaches a client how to experience and control sensations and responses
- Promotes self-regulation

You can utilize this approach in any of several ways, including on its own conversationally, as an induction, a deepener or at any point within the hypnotic session. I've even used it to bring people back out of hypnotic states!

Make sure a client understands the benefit of doing it frequently to retrain the brain and nervous system, along with creating comfort and peace.

Here's a template:

> Focus your attention on various parts of your body to balance body and mind and calm the autonomous nervous system, which is involved in stress, and the limbic system in the brain, which controls emotions.
>
> This process involves targeting your focus, imagining how you feel and repeating that thought three times.
>
> As you turn your attention to your arms, think to yourself: *"My arms are comfortably heavy"* Repeat...
>
> Then, think about how your legs feel: *"My legs are comfortably heavy"* Repeat...
>
> Next, consider how your chest and solar plexus feel: *"My solar plexus is comfortable"* Repeat...

Focus on your heartbeat: *"My heartbeat is calm and regular"* Repeat...

Think about your stomach: *"My stomach is soft and warm"* Repeat...

Bring your attention to your forehead: *"My forehead is cool and calm"* Repeat...

Notice how easy it was for you to feel calm and comfortable!

Regular use of autogenic training develops awareness and mastery of these calm and comfortable feelings, creating a positive reflex and promoting general wellness.

Object Imagery

It wouldn't be a proper hypnosis book without mention of the power of objectifying thoughts, emotions and sensations, so let me tell you that one of the most effective approaches you can use is Object Imagery.

Simply by systematically identifying a feeling, whether it is a physical sensation or an emotion, as if it were a specific thing, one can begin to gain a sense of control over it. The classic approach has us guiding a client into focusing in on the feeling, getting in touch with various sub-modalities, changing them and then deciding what they want to do with the end product.

Chronic pain often keeps people from being as physically active as they want, in addition to being a trigger for unhealthy eating or drinking. When working with such a case, begin by helping a client calibrate what they are feeling. You can use a pain scale or you might prefer to use a comfort scale to start reframing how a person actually thinks about the sensation. Once you both have a sense of the level of suffering, employ the imagination further:

Kelley: So, you told me that your back aches and that keeps you from taking a walk after dinner. Your doctor told you that walking will actually improve your back but you just can't get started when it feels that way. If you could reduce the suffering you experience, would you get out and take a walk?

Client: Sure. If I could walk even for ten or fifteen minutes without all that pain, that would be great!

Kelley: When you can walk for ten or fifteen minutes in a bit more comfort, that would be acceptable, then?

Client: Yes. I'd get more active, for sure.

Kelley: Good. Let's do that. I want you to close your eyes and get in touch with that sensation...that feeling that has been keeping you from walking until now. Let me know when you are aware of it...and describe it to me.

Client: It's in my lower back, just above my tailbone. I can feel the pressure of it even sitting here. Kind of a dull throb.

Kelley: Thank you. Now, just imagine that feeling...is a thing...an object of some shape...and I want you to let it appear right in front of you...like it's hovering in mid-air. Let me know when you see it.

Client: It's there.

Kelley: Okay. What shape is that object?

Client: It's a block.

Kelley: Interesting! Does it have a certain color to it?

Client: It's black.

Kelley: It's black. Good. How big is it? Can you show me with your hands?

Client gestures with hands.

Kelley: *And when you reach out and touch it, how does it feel? Is there a temperature to it?*

Client: *It's cold.*

Kelley: *It's cold. How about the consistency and texture? Is it firm and solid or is it pliable?*

Client: *It's like a rock. Hard and rough.*

Kelley: *Hard and rough, like a rock. Great. And, tell me...is that thing just suspended there like it's frozen...or is it moving in any way?*

Client: *It's just frozen.*

Kelley: *And what do you hear?*

Client: *Silent.*

Kelley: *Cool. How about we play with this feeling, this object, a bit? Can you think of a different, more comfortable shape...one you would prefer it take on?*

Client: *A ball?*

Kelley: *Yeah, a ball sounds good...would it be like a sports ball...or some other type of sphere shape?*

Client: *A Koosh ball.*

Kelley: *I love those! Can you turn it into a Koosh ball...now? What color will it be?*

Client: *It's multi-colored...warm colors like red and orange and a bit of purple.*

Kelley: *And what size will you make it become?*

Client shows a shrinking size with hands.

Kelley: *And is it still cold?*

Client: *No, I'm warming it up a bit.*

Kelley: *And how does it feel when you touch it?*

Client: *It's squishy and a bit fuzzy.*

Kelley: *Is there anything else you want to change about it?*

Client: *I'm making it smell good...like cinnamon.*

Kelley: *A cinnamon-scented Koosh ball...love it! And how does that feel to you now?*

Client smiles: *It feels pretty good.*

Kelley: *Wonderful. And you get to choose what you do with it now...you can put it back there where you got it from...or, you can let it go. I'll let you decide.*

Client: *Okay.*

Following this, re-calibrate how the client experiences the sensation and make sure they can replicate the exercise on their own if they need to. Discuss how Object Imagery might be used to stave off cravings, reduce unhelpful feelings and reactions. If your client has mentioned specific pitfalls in their life, ask them how they might use this technique to successfully navigate past or through them.

Tip: These type of conversations are essentially future pacing exercises that will equip the client with the knowledge and confidence that they can deal with any challenges ahead.

Metaphors for Weight Loss

We can go even further when we utilize a client's interests and passions to help them find relief from physical and emotional pain, fears, stress and even food cravings.

The power in using metaphor is that with it we create a direct conversation with the creative imagination, that part of the mind that is so influential in our perceptions and behaviors. When we think and speak rationally and logically about the very valid reasons for changing eating patterns, that inner mind doesn't generally pay much attention. It's when we activate more creative, colorful and emotional thoughts and ideas that it suddenly perks up and says, "Hey, that's interesting!"

Since one of the rules of the mind involves a tendency to resist that which we try to exhort, using a side door via metaphor can help gain access and cooperation in a subtle yet effective manner.

We can find metaphorical fodder all around us – in our daily experiences with conversation, books, songs and more. Once you tune your attention to the presence of metaphor, it abounds!

When it comes to using metaphors to help our weight loss clients, there are an unlimited amount of them. Some of the ways which we relate the work of losing weight and getting fit include:

The mind-body is a machine which needs to be maintained properly and without specific care, begins to break down.

Patter Box

> *Your body is the vehicle of your life.*

Food, and our relationship to it, is often a metaphor! We all know of certain associations with people, places and times in our life to a particular food. In fact, it's these associations, or anchors, that can be part of the problem when it comes to relying on "comfort foods" to feel better in some way.

156

These internal programs that are laid down in our early years can run in default for the rest of our lives, leading people to feel "stuck".

Or, how about this: "Let food be thy medicine." Anointing food with healing powers is an incredible influence that can be capitalized upon, as long as it's used ethically. As can the idea of "addiction", by the way. Although I've yet to meet a weight loss client who is addicted to broccoli, I sure have met a bunch who claim to be addicted to bread, sweets and chocolate! Think about the meaning of that confession and how it keeps a person trapped or feeling victimized and helpless.

This leads us into another metaphor: the mind-body as a computer that can be re-programmed. References to switching on or off certain preferences, for example, make it seem as simple as flipping a toggle on a mechanical device.

Even descriptions such as "re-wiring", referring to brain plasticity, conjures up a certain imagery that leads clients to believe we are master electricians who can repair circuits that have become broken or entangled.

Excess weight itself is sometimes compared to being:

- a heavy burden
- a protective layer or some type of insulation
- the physical manifestation of unresolved feelings
- the result of having "stuffed" one's emotions

The journey to better health through weight loss is rife with metaphor: the path to success; the road to follow, stick to, or avoid falling off.

Metaphors that can be unhelpful incite feelings of guilt and shame:

In this day and age, it's pretty much impossible to only consume items that support weight loss so when a person succumbs to what is perceived as "bad behavior", they suffer from that judgment and struggle even more to create a healthy relationship with food.

When judgement is served on a plate along with food, things get even more interesting. How often have you thought or said, "This food is good...and that one is bad?" How often have you heard a client say, "I was bad yesterday," referring to having eaten something unhealthy?

Metaphors of saintliness or sinfulness add to those layers of guilt over eating choices...further compounding feelings of failure and hopelessness for obese and overweight people.

A war frame can also frustrate and exhaust a client. Having to keep up the "fight" by attending to a diet and then feeling like they have lost the battle reminds them of all their past failures. Even more importantly, this type of mindset can pit a person against their own body...which rarely does any good.

As always, when working in a client-centered manner, pay close attention to the presence of metaphors and how they are helping or hurting. This is a great place to infuse a sense of fun into your work – even getting silly or ridiculous can transform the meaning of what and how your client is doing!

Note: When I refer to having fun, being silly, etc., I want to emphasize that these attitudes involve laughing with your client, not at them.

I'll offer a great example of how using the metaphorical power of one simple word can transform the way your client looks at exercise in the next chapter.

Chapter Ten   Getting Moving

Exercise. This word makes a lot of weight loss clients cringe. For those people who naturally love the feeling of being physically active, it's difficult to understand how others can become so sedentary. After all, it's recently been suggested that sitting is the new smoking – it's just that dangerous to be underactive for hours at a time, day in and day out.

The truth is that many of our weight loss clients suffer from inadequate levels of physical activity and just as important, they have low levels of motivation when it comes to getting the body moving. They have many reasons for this, of course, including:

- chronic pain that limits their movements
- lack of energy due to unhealthy eating/sleeping habits
- limiting beliefs about the value and enjoyment of exercise
- their own beliefs about not being an "athletic person"
- lack of support and company in physical activities
- no ideas about the kind of things they can realistically do

As you can see, all of these excuses are ones that we can help them overcome. I usually begin with helping a person change any limiting thoughts or beliefs they have around the topic of exercise. This can start with simply reframing the word, "exercise", which is problematic for so many.

By merely suggesting that we no longer think or refer to physical activity as "exercise" but instead, use the word, "recess", things instantly begin to feel better. Most clients smile and nod, remembering how they enjoyed recess as a child...perhaps even remember that they used to enjoy running, skipping, climbing and all of those other activities that children naturally love.

Occasionally, you will have a client who wasn't physically active as a child and that's okay. You can reassure them that in hypnosis, their inner child will finally get the chance to come out and play. Or, if recess does not hold positive associations for some reason, such as a memory of being bullied or feeling isolated, you can easily release that word and take a different tack. Being an effective hypnotist means that you can think on your feet, even while sitting with a client, and be flexible.

For those with whom the idea of recess resonates, you can begin to utilize the power of that word right away and ask how the client imagines taking a recess during their typical day. Some clients might still frown and have difficulty coming up with an answer, but many will be skipping ahead, mentioning that they could get outside and take a walk, they could try some yoga, they could go swimming, etc.

Our goal is to elicit at least a couple of ways (choice leads to control) that the client can get moving. These activities need to be realistic and achievable, something that can be accessed and maintained without involving a lot of extra time, effort or money. Otherwise, they just won't be sustainable, even if the client does get started.

And for people who have been inactive for extended periods of time, small changes are best. This means creating goals of walking for as short a period of time as 10-15 minutes to begin with, gradually adding to that as strength grows. A formula for increasing functional exercise can goes something like:

Day 1	10 min	Day 2	15 min
Day 3	10 min	Day 4	15 min
Day 5	15 min	Day 6	10 min
Day 7	15 min	Day 8	20 min

This resembles how growth usually happens for a person, with advances and returns – never just in a straight incline, but accommodating for rest periods while staying on the path. I never prescribe the specific exercise nor the amount of time, but help the client explore options and decide for themselves what, when and how they will engage in it. Then, I use those details as fodder for hypnotic suggestions within our sessions.

This is also an great place to utilize "The Promise" strategy I presented in Chapter Four, by the way!

Modelling an Active Lifestyle

Most everyone knows, either personally or otherwise, someone who engages in regular physical activity and even makes it look natural and enjoyable. This might be a friend or family member or it may be a celebrity or sports hero. Find out who your client admires in this regard and ask them specifically to describe what it is about the role model that they appreciate.

If you have studied NLP, you may be familiar with an approach called "Circle of Excellence", which is an effective way to implement modelling. Another that I learned from my original hypnosis instructor, Ron Stubbs, is one I call "The Golden Rings" and I include it in the Script Appendix at the end of this book. You'll see that it's quite adaptable for changing behavior and adopting helpful habits, whether those are related to eating or physical activity...or even how a person feels about themselves.

Take Your Client There Physically

One of the biggest evolutions in my hypnosis practice in recent years has been my liberation from an "office mindset". I worked hard to create an ideal office setting in which to help people - so ideal, in fact - that it didn't dawn on me for quite some time that I can help my clients in just about any place. I was stuck in my office mindset!

If you have a weight loss client who is having a hard time deciding what physical activity is right for them, or, they just haven't been able to muster the gumption to start moving, you can help them by getting moving with them.

Since my revelation, I have enjoyed countless walks with clients around my office neighborhood – often just for 10 minutes or so, but this is long enough for them to get experience of having a good time while walking. As we walk, I am looking for opportunities to anchor the positive feelings we are creating to the walking activity, using gestures, words and even songs.

I have met clients for sessions at swimming pools, at the gym, and at the high school track. I love to get out and visit these places, so it's a win for both of us.

I'm even now offering hypnosis in the outdoors – I am fortunate to live in a gorgeous part of the world and when I can take a client on a gentle hike along the coast, all is well. A "forest bathing" session is restorative even as it is physical. I know that these types of experiences resonate and uplift my clients in many ways.

So, feel free to get active with your clients, in ways that they will respond positively to, and you will see them blossom.

Another way to inspire a weight loss client to get active is to match them up with another of your clients (with both of their permission). Having a walking buddy can make a huge difference to the consistency and commitment of being physically active. At the very least, you can help your client find an area resource, such as a walking club.

Chapter Eleven   Making Adjustments

Even when things appear to go wrong, I usually remind myself that everything is actually right. Being able to let go of judgment of something being "good" or "bad" is a gift that helps us not only accept life's trials but move more easily through them.

Over the years, I have turned into a bit of a Reframe Queen and know that I can make lemonade out of just about anything. I strive to teach my clients how to do that, too, even as they are moving toward making improvements in their lives.

This is different than telling someone to "think positive" – it's been shown that pressuring people, especially those who have been suffering with chronic depression and other long term problems, to simply use affirmations just doesn't work. In fact, it can make them feel worse as, once again, they fail.

Instead, I encourage fostering a positive mindset and teach my clients how to systematically life themselves out of ruts with fun and easy hypnotic exercises. Even a simple "Laugh Out Loud" at life's irritations and disappointments can do the trick as long as it's conducted on a regular basis (entrainment leads to victory).

I've encountered clients whose eating habits had been unhealthy for years and even though they were changing them, the weight still stuck. When the scale hasn't budged an ounce in two weeks, despite having let go of eating processed food and otherwise making positive changes, it's disappointing. I assure clients who aren't having quick results, especially those who had particularly poor diets and or high levels of stress, that it can take a while for the body to adjust and progress may indeed be hampered during this stage.

I also suggest that by our next appointment, there will probably be a more positive response. If there is not, chances are that the client is not following the guidelines and doing their part.

Additionally, skewed perceptions can fool us into thinking that we are missing out on success. I recall one weight loss client who stormed into her second appointment with me, mad as a bee. She stood in front of me, hands on hips and said, "This isn't working!" So, I invited her to sit down and tell me about her week.

She went on to say, "Well, on Thursday I went to that fast food place..." (This was one of the habits we were hoping to break.) "And I ordered this turkey sandwich thing. It tasted like cardboard and I couldn't eat it."

I sat quietly, waiting, and it didn't take long for her to realize that of course, it was working, just maybe not in the way she had expected.

"Oh," she said and then started giggling. What followed then was one very powerful session.

Saboteurs

We have all met them – those people who, thinking that they are being kind and helpful, are actually waylaying our progress, undermining our confidence and determination as we strive for improvement. A client may describe them in fond terms or they may have a built-up resentment for the power that such people of influence hold over them.

In some cases, a spouse or partner may not be enthused about the client's weight loss based upon their own fears and insecurities. Some people worry about being left behind when a family member wakes up and starts taking better care of themselves.

One of the big challenges clients have lies in being able to stick to their guns when in the company of others who don't care about healthy eating. My father, long ago, told me, "Look at your friends to see yourself." And yes, research bears out that if a person hang out often with overweight friends, their own eating habits and weight will likely be influenced in a way that will cause them to also become or remain overweight. Even if they resist that peer pressure, they are often subjected to scorn, rejection and expressions of doubt in their ability to lose weight.

Once again, self-empowerment is the name of the game and we want to find creative ways to equip our clients with the ability to not only resist but to self-regulate against any potential outside sabotage that keeps them from achieving their weight loss and health goals. One of the tricks to doing this successfully is to help a client achieve independence of thought and action *without* alienating them from the people in their life who do have value to them.

I have found one of the best courses to accomplish this is through the development and use of a protective device. When I provide a client with one, they not only feel safe and protected, they also become more able to shift perspective, which shifts the way that they feel about perceived "attacks" and other negative energies.

While this tool can help protect and defend a weight loss client against pressures from others to join them in unhealthy eating or from feeling guilty because they are not participating, it can also insulate them from temptations that in the past would have overpowered them.

An effective protective shield can help a person establish and maintain boundaries (a valued component of any ego-strengthening protocol) while also giving them an expanded perspective...so that they can then make a choice about how, when and where they are responding. And, once again, we know that having a sense of choice leads to a sense of control.

Tip: You will find my script for a protective shield in the Script Appendix at the end of this book.

Mastering Plateaus

So, your client has been doing well and releasing a steady amount of weight at a healthy rate. (Two to three pounds a week, for the average overweight adult, is a weight loss level that is usually safe and provides a good chance for sustainability.) Then, you get a phone call or email that indicates they are stuck – it's been sometime since the scale budged and they are stressed over the stalling. What to do?!

The very first thing to do is to reassure your client that it's perfectly normal to have pauses in the weight loss. Think about it: especially if a body has been dealing with excess weight, once changes are made it's a bit of a shock. The natural inclination can be for it to react as if there is a famine, reserving resources to get through the cold winter. The answer to this is perseverance – you must convince your client not to panic or get discouraged and to keep on their path of healthy eating and increased physical activity.

A helpful hypnotic process at this point involves future pacing. Giving your client some short term glimpses into what will come as they continue to attend to their new behaviors can build confidence that they will eventually start to release weight again. I like to utilize short term goals because they align with our cultural preference for instant results.

For example, I recently worked with a woman who came to me in dire straits – she was nearly 200 pounds overweight and had several physical challenges that were directly related to her obesity, namely, breathing difficulties, joint pain and elevated blood sugar levels.

Within a month, she had released nearly 20 pounds and was already feeling better. But, as the holidays neared, her weight loss stopped and she felt like she was in danger of going backwards. Our fourth session involved calming her panic and giving her a peek into her life in the spring time where she was comfortably walking in the local tulip fields...lighter and happier.

166

Sure enough, after a week or so, my client's weight loss started up again. Once she was able to stop worrying, which is tantamount to praying for something unwanted to happen, her body naturally got back on the healing path.

Another tactic is to actually employ the metaphor of a plateau for these clients. Somewhere in the hypnotic session, I lift them up in a flying experience, where they are cruising along a beautiful savannah...observing the land below as they move forward along a seemingly endless plateau. I use language that resonates with the individual and especially with their favored representational system, although I have found that never to be just one so I hit them all, just in case!

At some point, the client is launched off the edge of the plateau, safely into mid-air where they are free to fly, soar, drift...leaving that weight behind them. From here, we might move along the skyline to the future or elsewhere, further enhancing the experience.

Again, utilize who your client is and what they love to get things moving. I used a metaphor of a snowball rolling down the mountain, gaining unstoppable momentum, for a client who loved to ski. A golfing client responded well when I suggested that he mentally yell, "Fore!" to announce to the world that he was about to let loose of another pound. Have fun with it and your clients will ride along with your creativity and enthusiasm, reframing those old weight loss plateaus to opportunities for movement.

Patter Box

> *It can become natural and easy to finish all that one starts. A sense of pride in completing tasks and projects can grow. A feeling of quiet satisfaction in a job well done can be its own reward.*
> ~ Sherry Hood

Chapter Twelve   Using Self Hypnosis

Yes, the regular practice of brief bouts of self-hypnosis create profound improvements in a person's state of mind and being, automatically aiding in the release of unwanted, excess weight. But we can also utilize these "recesses" during our life to make positive internal suggestions that promote improvement on a variety of levels.

I use a simple technique that will activate the Relaxation Response and then add something special to it. When we explain to a client that moving into these self-directed states of relaxation also provides access to the subconscious, it becomes clear to them that they can also use this time to input positive suggestions.

Auto Suggestion

Most clients are familiar with affirmations and they may even say that they've tried using them and they didn't work. I will acknowledge their efforts and say, "Great! Now you are going to learn why that didn't work so well..." and then explain to them how gaining direct access to the subconscious is so important.

The biggest limitation to using affirmations is that they mostly involve conscious intention and fail to really involve the subconscious realm. And, as mentioned earlier, when attempted use of these positive assertions is done by people who are depressed or otherwise stuck in chronic states, they can actually do the opposite and make them feel worse! After reciting an affirmation daily without seeing any results, many people become discouraged and tell themselves that they have once again failed at something that apparently works for everyone else. And this results in driving even more of the emotional hunger responses.

A little later, I will give details in how I teach a client to apply helpful suggestions within a self-hypnosis exercise. But first, let's talk about how to best structure an effective suggestion. The following are some guidelines which will help you not only create powerful suggestions and affirmations but you can teach them to your client so that they will be empowered to do so, too.

I'll use a client's desire to get physically active as a target to develop an effective suggestion using the guidelines:

1. Use the Present Tense

Many weight loss clients have been living in a state where they are always waiting to start their improvement. They promise themselves that they are going to start a diet on Monday, or after the holidays or as soon as visiting company leaves.

The subconscious realm really doesn't care about time – time is suspended and all experience is currently available as if it is happening. To activate a suggestion within the subconscious, speak that same time-language and frame it *as if it is happening.* Otherwise, the desired suggestion will just be something else, waiting to occur.

So, instead of thinking, "*I am going to walk every day,*" a more effective statement would be, "*I love walking every day!*"

2. Include Specifics in a Positive Way

Even as you are using the present tense, you want to be specific about the when, where, how, etc.

"*You feel fantastic when you go for a walk around your neighborhood with your dog, every Friday evening after dinner, between 5 and 8 pm.*"

Tip: Some research says that the mind responds best to a range, providing a bit of wiggle room.

Using terms like, "I am" or "I feel" is more effective than "I will", just as referring to past behaviors can be counter-productive. Avoid creating suggestions that mention no longer doing something you want to change. Instead, focus on language and subsequent imagery of the desired changes in behavior and attitude that will support your goals.

Break down your goals into steps and make suggestions for each of them. Instead of framing your goal as, "I am becoming healthy so my clothing fits comfortably," try, "I feel great as I tighten my belt into the skinnier setting." And, of course, make sure that the goal is realistic because just like a savvy teen, your inner mind will deduce whether it's actually doable.

3. Keep it Simple

The part of your mind you want to reach is really pretty childlike and takes things literally. You don't need fancy language here, so avoid lengthy, technical or psychological terms.

4. Make it Exciting

My clients usually laugh when I demonstrate how the inner mind responds to things like, "*I like to eat brussels sprouts because they are good for me.*" Halfway through that affirmation I start to snore. But, when we say something like, "*I get a thrill when I enjoy some beautiful, tasty, energizing brussels sprouts!*" we know that the subconscious mind is intrigued and paying better attention. After all, isn't that how the food industry does it?

5. Activate Your Suggestion

Not only do you want the words to imply action, doing and being, but you want them to incorporate a plan of action. This might be a suggestion for eating mindfully, walking after dinner, drinking a glass of water first thing in the morning, etc. Consider it as a living thing that is fueling success by promoting automatic action on a deep level.

6. Make it Personal

Only when a person realizes and accepts that no one and nothing else can make them do anything, will they take personal responsibility. And since personal responsibility is required for making permanent lifestyle changes, letting go of blame or dependency on others is important. Neither will others change due to our own suggestions, although many people do find those around them shifting in accordance to what is happening.

7. Use Your Own Name

Yes – when you talk to yourself, apparently you listen better! I like to create positive suggestions that commend me for doing well, such as, "Hey Kelley, I like the way you just _____!" This is such a wonderful counter to decades of negative self-talk, breaking those unhelpful patterns. Everyone should choose to do it.

8. Be Positive

I'm repeating myself here because it's really important. Use words that support and inspire instead of words that chastise or restrict. For example, ditch the "I have to...", "I need...", "I must...", "I should..." and even the "I want...". Instead, substitute my favorite, freeing word, "choose". It's pretty empowering – try it now for yourself.

Patter Box

> *I choose to nurture my healthy body with delicious and nutritious food in just the right amount...at just the right time...*

Using Self Hypnosis to Program Your Suggestion

I learned from Roger Moore a nice little tip: pick up some packs of 3 x 5 colored index cards from your local dollar store. After teaching your client a quick self-hypnosis process and explaining how to construct effective suggestions, give them a pack of the cards.

Suggest that they assign a different color for each area of their life goals; for example: green for food intake, blue for exercise, pink for rest and relaxation, yellow for healthy social interactions, etc.

Once they have a bunch of positive suggestions listed on their cards, they can, each day, select one of the cards and have the suggestion on it be the focus of their self-hypnosis for that day.

This is a great way to utilize EFT, by the way! Picking one topic to tap on a day, a person can systematically address an unlimited number of issues or challenges in a manageable way.

Ideomotor Pendulum Work

There are many reasons why it is beneficial to introduce a client to this method of mind-body communication. One of the goals in hypnotherapy is to enhance the ability of a person to pay attention to their inner mind, so providing them with one more tool reinforces the value of that and also motivates them, in a fun and private way, to continue self-exploration.

A weight loss client may use a pendulum to determine how they are feeling about change, discover current beliefs, help with decision-making, explore blocks to success or even relocate a lost object!

More than one of my clients have kept their pendulum in their pocket or purse, taking it out at mealtime to determine if and how hungry they actually are. You can imagine how using it enhances mindfulness when it comes to eating.

Clients can test out auto-suggestions to make sure that they are congruent with their subconscious. For example, perhaps they are using self-hypnosis to input the thought, "I enjoy eating healthy vegetables at every meal." Since the part of our mind that is being implored to help the client by leading them to eat more healthy is very literal, it may find "eating vegetables at every meal" unsuitable in some way. A check with a pendulum can determine if a suggestion is appropriate and acceptable; if not, it can be adjusted until a positive response is given.

Here's how I teach a client to use a pendulum:

> 1. To find your "yes" swing direction, ask a simple, brief question that would only prompt a "yes" reply. (For example: "Is my name Kelley?") Wait for the object to swing in a distinct direction, then record on the paper that motion with arrows. Stop the motion and take a breath, clearing your mind.

> 2. Ask a question to elicit a "no" answer. (Am I a male? – for a female, of course!) Record the swing direction.

> 3. Establish an answer of "I don't know" IDK (What is the temperature in Helsinki?)

> 4. Establish an answer of "I don't want to say" IDWTS (Think of a tender or painful issue that you would rather not consider...)

To use the pendulum for self-discovery work, you can be a "detective" of sorts. First, ask if it is okay to be doing this work and wait for a "yes" indication. If you receive a "no", this is a sign that the subconscious is resisting strongly and you may want to address some lighter topics for a couple of days to establish trust. (Crazy, huh, that our own SC doesn't trust ourselves?!)

If you receive a "yes" reply, proceed. Think of WHO, WHEN, WHERE, WHAT and WHY to track down information. You can begin by thinking about your trouble or issue and asking first, "Is anyone else involved in this problem", meaning does anyone else influence or promote it? Depending on the response, you can follow that or move on to the next, "Did I first experience this before the age of _____?" This way you can track down a time or origin, even a location.

Often, at some point in the discovery process, memories flood up and enlightenment happens! Be sure to keep your questions clear and simple. I was once investigating why I was blocked in a certain area of my life and the answers led me to something that happened in my house. I went from room to room, with no resolution...until I suddenly realized that it was not my CURRENT house, but the one I lived in previously, years ago.

The SC does not distinguish the past from the present; it's all the same to it, so you need be specific. Think very literally, like a child, and you will have success in communicating with your SC!

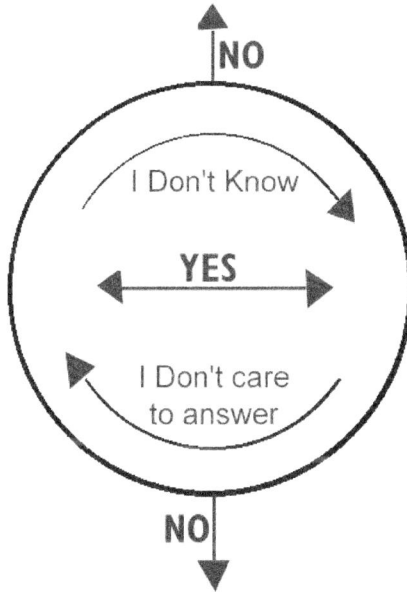

After teaching a client how to use a pendulum, I give them these guidelines to take home with their new super cool tool.

Pendulum Guidelines

1. Establish your answer key (the preceding diagram is an example, your pattern may be different!)

YES =

NO =

I DON'T KNOW =

I DON"T WANT TO SAY =

2. Ask simple and clear questions

3. Answers come from your subconscious

4. Be patient; allow time for response

5. Be a detective: When, Where, Who, What, and sometimes...Why

6. Limit session to 60 mins.

7. Practice makes better

8. Have fun!

Tip: I often run teen workshops and one of our favorite activities is to put together pendulums and then learn how to use them. Imagine helping overweight teens learn how powerful their minds are!

Hypnosis Recordings

As you know, one of the ways that we learn new patterns and habits is through repetition. This is why I always give my clients hypnosis recordings to listen to between our sessions. The featured topics will range from specific weight loss suggestions to stress reduction, sleep enhancement, etc.

There have been times when, for one reason or another, a client hasn't been able to start working with me for weight loss right away. In such a case, I have sent them a hypnosis for relaxation recording to start priming their mind for our eventual work. These clients are shocked to discover that after merely listening to the recording for a week or so, they begin to experience shifts in attitudes, behavior and even weight! But you and I aren't surprised by that in the least, are we?!

So, you will want to have at least a couple of recordings to share with your clients. I recommend that you create them yourself because listening to their hypnotherapist will not only continue to align your client to you, it will anchor your voice even more firmly as a positive guide for improvement.

I use the free program, Audacity. It's easy to learn – there are many tutorials online!

In the Appendix at the back of this book, I've included scripts for a general relaxation experience, a couple of progressive weight loss recordings and also a sleep/pain relief script. And if you really want to serve your client well, consider making a custom recording just for them that incorporates what you know they need to hear.

Chapter Thirteen   Couples and Groups

This chapter deals with how we can help multiple clients, individually and together, achieve their goals while taking advantage of the group dynamic.

Couples

It's not unusual to get requests from couples of all sorts – married or otherwise partnered, mother and daughter, sisters, etc. – who want to utilize hypnosis together for weight loss. Particularly for people who live together, it can be very helpful to have company and support in making the desired lifestyle changes.

Note: This can, however, be a grey area for non-licensed hypnotists who are not qualified for couples' or family counseling. Be sure to stay within your scope of practice and refer out when needed.

I offer a "couples program" for partners who want to lose weight. Currently, a pre-paid, 6 session program costs $1000 for an individual client. Couples who sign up together and pre-pay enjoy an additional discount, making the total fee $1800.

I structure the sessions in this way:

> Our first session is comprised of a pre-talk and initial intake with both clients present. After about 30 minutes, one steps out into my comfortable waiting room while I continue with further, more personal intake for the other. This is followed by creating the foundation for our work through further conversational hypnosis/NLP and a formal hypnosis experience.
>
> I repeat this process with the second partner. Total time spent with the couple in this first encounter is usually three hours. (Later ones are usually shorter – approx.. 2 hours.)

Subsequent sessions are conducted similarly: both people spend some time, giving feedback to me, discussing how things are going. I usually have some tool that I will introduce to them, such as an anchor collapse, an assessment, etc. I encourage them to use it and share the experience with each other on their own time.

The couple then separate and I work individually with them. By the way, I let them choose who is to do that first and once they decide, they usually stay with that pattern.

Sometimes, following the course of sessions, one (or both) may opt to continue on their own and I extend the same discounted session fee.

Now, while spending time explaining, exploring, and teaching with both people present is an economic expenditure of time, there is something even more valuable in doing this. Observing the dynamic between the couple will provide insight and direction, assisting you in making your work even more effective.

One couple, who were obviously very much in love with each other, couldn't decide which of them would first experience hypnosis with me. But they weren't afraid – they each wanted the other to go first as a gift! I realized that these two were very giving people...and was later able to utilize that sense of self-sacrifice while strengthening their motivation to lose weight and get healthier.

Another, older, married couple came to me for help. He was quite obese, while she wanted only to lose about 20 pounds or so. It was apparent that she came along for the ride primarily to support her husband, who had been trying to eat himself to death. A quiet, subdued woman, his wife didn't have much belief in what we were about to do and it was my job to turn that around. Watching the sense of martyrdom that she displayed about her husband told me that she might welcome some "selfish" attention and I was right. Within our private sessions, she found her sense of autonomy while her husband moved through his own limitations, both achieving their weight loss goals. Later, my male client confessed that for the first time in decades, he and his wife had resumed sexual relations!

A mother and her daughter signed up for weight loss sessions together and were able to use their close relationship as a resource to keep each other on track. They shared a wonderful sense of humor and together decided to laugh every time either of them had an unhealthy craving. I wish I could have been in their home as they dealt with the cravings!

Note: Client confidentiality is vital when working with couples of any kind. If a couple wants to share their experiences with each other, that's their business. I never do, nor do I acknowledge anything about one to the other, even when they are fishing for details!

Groups

There is a certain power in numbers. One of the common challenges of people who struggle with their weight, especially as they age, is that of feeling isolated. This can be based on actual or imagined perceptions of low self-worth, of feeling discriminated against or otherwise rejected and it can also be coming from the very real situation of living alone without a reliable and healthy support system.

An amazing thing happens when these people find that they are not the only one who struggles with weight: a degree of self-blame and self-doubt is lightened. They begin to feel that they may be part of something bigger than just themselves. Now, in some cases, this can become unhelpful: research shows that one's friends have a big influence on one's eating choices, making it even more important to make connections with others who share weight loss goals.

For people who don't have friends or family and have just been languishing alone, eating for company, the idea of connecting with others on the same path can be appealing. And, working with a group of people for weight loss can be fun, providing you are confident and able to manage the different personalities that may be present.

Here's how I promote and conduct group weight loss programs:

Periodically, I post on Craigslist and with strategically-placed flyers around town, that I am holding a Group Weight Loss Event at my hypnosis center. I usually schedule it near the first or the middle of the month (pay periods for many) and promote it about 3 weeks ahead of time.

I offer a 3-hour program for $30 per person ($25 each for couples). Charging a nominal price adds value to attendance, even though people would happily come to a free event, I want to pre-screen potential future clients for motivation. Spending their hard-earned dollars often indicates a higher level of motivation.

Points to include in promotional materials:

- Topic
- Date
- Location
- Brief reference/statistic regarding how hypnosis helps with weight loss
- What attendees will get/experience/learn
- Cost
- How to register
- Mini-bio about me

I create a special page on my website, complete with a PayPal button for people to pre-register. When I have received their registration, I contact them and confirm, asking them to let me know if they have any specific questions or information I need to know. A surprising amount of people do write back to me and this creates a personal connection so that by the time we meet at the actual event, rapport is instantly present. I've also had a few parties decide not to attend the event and instead apply their registration fee toward private sessions with me.

Which brings us to the very reason to throw these types of gatherings: three hours gives us enough time to demonstrate and provide experiential lessons of the power of hypnosis. Many people who are considering using hypnosis may be hesitant because they've never actually met a hypnotist in person and probably don't understand how it all works. Perhaps they are leery because they have already failed with other weight loss attempts and they don't want to fail again; or they are afraid of being taken advantage of or otherwise tricked.

A fun experience, meeting other like-minded individuals with similar challenges, can change all of that. Even if an attendee doesn't take advantage of any "sign up now discount" for private sessions, chances are that you will hear from them in the future.

I limit this program to 8 people – mainly because that's the most I can comfortably accommodate in my group session room but also because that's a number that I feel adept giving personal attention to. There's no reason why that number can't be doubled...or tripled.

Some of the components I include in this type of event:

- Brief introduction of myself, topic
- Self-introduction of attendees
- Explanation of hypnosis and why it can help with weight loss
- Discussion of various influences on weight
- Experiential lesson creating a positive resource anchor
- Feedback from participants
- Work with a volunteer and demonstrate anchor collapse technique
- Help attendees create mental blueprint for what they want to achieve

- Guide them in future pacing exercise
- Discussion

Potential problems when working with a group:

1) Although the attendees have paid in money and time to learn from you, there may be one (or more) who is skeptical and insists on challenging what you are sharing. These types of people can easily highjack your presentation, damaging belief and expectation within the entire group...if you so allow it. It's imperative that, if an attendee begins to argue or present stories or opinions that are contrary to what you are saying, you stop them and let them know you are happy to discuss that with them later. Although it doesn't happen often, this is a good tactic that will keep the momentum of your event going in a positive direction.

Another approach is to acknowledge what the person is saying and then re-direct it immediately. An example:

Suppose an attendee says that someone they know tried hypnosis and it didn't work. Your response can be that yes, hypnosis only works for most people and you suspect that the people who are present are going to be able to engage on some level. In fact, you can add the observation that those who are a bit more intelligent or creative are usually more responsive. You can then move on to demonstrate with a simple magnetic fingers exercise and watch everyone respond beautifully!

2) Attendees take over the presentation. The group dynamic may be so welcoming that people start to share their stories at length, cutting into your program. One young woman suddenly burst into tears and blurted out details of her past sexual abuse, making a few people visibly uncomfortable. This type of situation can be easily handled by offering to speak privately with the party following the event.

It takes finesse to maintain control of your group. One way to prevent "conversational high-jacking" is to tell the group up front: "I am going to present some information and then later, I will ask for questions or comments. Please wait until that time to contribute unless I specifically ask. Thanks!"

3) People refuse to participate. This can happen! If you are conducting a guided imagery, don't be surprised if not everyone closes their eyes. You can give the group permission to either engage with eyes closed...or not. Remember, it's not a test (although you are getting lots of clues from your attendees about their willingness and responsiveness) and if you are adept, you'll be able to entice even a reluctant attendee to step into their hypnotic self...even for a little while. Just go with the flow and refrain from commenting about anything that isn't happening, while focusing on the positive changes you observe and feel.

4) Interruptions. Cell phones ring, people need to cough, sneeze or use the bathroom, someone arrives late – that's life. Do what you can to insure these things won't distract the group by asking ahead of time for compliance, but if they still happen, either ignore or utilize them. I once had a lady drop her entire purse contents onto the floor, which made a big racket. I paused, looked at the assortment and then looked back at her, saying, "That must be a big relief! Can you imagine that releasing weight is just that easy?!" Everyone cracked up and a couple of weeks later, in a private session, the same lady happily showed me her smaller, lighter handbag.

5) Staying on schedule. You are the only one that can make that happen, so start your program on time, even if everyone has not yet arrived. We teach people how to treat us and if latecomers notice that you aren't going to wait for them, that's a good lesson. Have a timeframe for each stage of your presentation and stick to it, within reason. If you don't want

to be distracted watching the clock, employ someone to do it for you, giving you signals to keep you on track. You can even use a time-keeping app on your phone or computer that will ring a soft chime at specific times.

Be sure to end your event punctually – it's very annoying to attend a meeting that goes beyond its advertised duration, especially if you have family or friends waiting elsewhere!

Handouts and other class materials:

You will want to have some things prepared ahead of time, including:

A sign-in sheet. Although you probably already have your attendees' contact information, the simple act of signing in helps to create a sense of inclusion and commitment. And, perhaps they have brought someone else along with them; "extra" guests often show up!

Means to process payments, not only for extra attendees, but for anyone taking advantage of any products you have for sale or even purchasing private hypnosis sessions.

Handouts related to any topics or lessons. These might be directions for a technique you taught, lists of area resources like gyms and pools, helpful weblinks, or any other idea you want to stick in a person's mind.

Products you have for sale such as recordings, books, etc. Clearly post prices for these things and have them at a separate table near your entrance. You can also offer a coupon for discounted private sessions.

Have bottles of water on hand. Besides a single raisin, I don't provide coffee, wine or any snacks of any kind to these people!

Props that you may incorporate in your work (these are all mentioned previously within this book):

> ~I sometimes invite participants to select a smooth stone for an anchoring exercise – we find a "power' word in hypnosis, anchoring a rubbing of the stone in their hand to the positive responses created by the word. Later they write the word on their stone with an indelible marker. I find my stones at a local beach but you can buy them at craft stores, too.

> ~A container of golden raisins. These are used in a mindful eating training. Wait until you are ready to start the experience before distributing them!

> ~Templates for The Wheel of Life exercise, along with colored felt pens.

> ~Pendulums and a simple sheet of directions.

Multiple class group programs work, as well. A series of weekly, short (60 - 90 minutes) sessions in which you address a certain aspect of hypnosis for weight loss is a great experience. You can structure the sessions very much as you would your individual program, dealing with the specific influences on weight systematically, adjusting them accordingly to your participant's needs.

Typical fees for 4 to 6 week programs like this can range from $150 to $300, depending on your market. And, you will find that, although people are attending the weekly sessions, they may also be interested in a private session with you to deal with more personal issues. You may even include a private session as part of the program – it's your deal and you can do it how you want. Just be clear and make it easy for a potential client to understand what you are offering.

Appendix of Scripts and Forms

Take a Trip to Your Perfect Place © Kelley T. Woods 2017

Induction of choice

Deepener

> *And you are just about to arrive in a very special place...a place that belongs just to you. This may be a place that you know from your past...maybe it's a place you know currently,...or, it may be a place that you are about to discover for the first time...right here...right now...I don't know...but what I do know... is that in this perfect place of yours exists everything that you desire...that you deserve...a sense of peace and well-being...of security...confidence...good health...*
>
> *One...go ahead...step into it now...begin to explore everything here that makes you feel so relaxed...so at ease...Use all of your senses to take it all in...Notice, is it daytime...or nighttime? What's the temperature like...any scenery? Shapes? Colors?*
>
> *Perhaps there are sounds...or music.*
>
> *A fragrance...aroma...*
>
> *Feel free to touch or taste anything that you desire...it all belongs to you.*
>
> *And notice how vast this perfect place is...it's unlimited, limited only by your imagination, which is limitless. In fact, please notice that over there...you will find a container, a receptacle of some type. Perhaps it's a box...or a basket...maybe a trunk...or a closet. And when you open it, you see that it is empty.*
>
> *But it is more than big enough, more than large enough to hold*

all of your worries...all of your concerns...anything that keeps you from feeling at peace will fit in here. And the great thing is that you don't even have to do an inventory of what those things are...your subconscious knows. It also knows that they will be safe here. You can always come back and get them later, if you choose to...or, you may decide to leave them there, knowing that you will be able to deal with anything you need to...calmly, effectively...from your improved state of mind.

So, for now, take those things off and place them into that container...notice how good that feels...how much lighter and easier you feel...close it up. You can even lock it and put the key in your pocket.

Now let yourself move further into this wonderful place of yours...find a spot where you can really relax...maybe a scene or a sensation that you know makes you so comfortable...even a little drowsy...or perhaps a bit of a floating, drifting feeling that is safe...secure...and you do feel good knowing that there really is nothing else that you need to be doing right now...no one asking anything of you except just this...that's right...

Notice how very relaxed and at ease you are right now...understand that you have effectively allowed a relaxation response to occur...you have moved your physical body into a healing state...so that its natural tendency toward homeostasis – that inclination to balance – is happening, without you even having to attend to it. What a gift to give to yourself! Wouldn't it be wonderful to do this on a regular basis? Perhaps daily or even more often...not just when you are stressed or uncomfortable...but to stay ahead of excess stress and tension? That would be nice, wouldn't it?

I'm going to show you how to do that...Please select one of your hands. It may be the left hand or it may be the right hand; the left hand may be the right hand...whichever is right for you, let the thumb and index finger on that hand begin to move toward each other...until they touch and begin to press lightly.

Wait until the client's fingertips touch.

Good. Now, as you apply a bit of pressure there, take three of those deep, slow breaths. And, you may even want to think of a word that denotes this peaceful feeling you are experiencing...perhaps it's the word, Peace, or maybe, Relax...maybe it's some other word that is even more personal to you.

As you breathe, think of that word...what you are now doing is embedding, deep into your subconscious, that whenever you press those fingertips together, take those deep breaths and think that word, all of these wonderful, peaceful feelings will come flooding into your mind and your body. And the more often you do this, the more natural and easy this will become...so that...before you know it, you will find that you spend more and more time in a calm and comfortable state of being.

Of course, it's interesting to realize that your body is like a robot...which your mind commands. I wonder what you will notice when you begin to apply a bit more pressure to those fingertips, in a pumping or pulsing motion...signaling your brain to release even more of those feel-good neurochemicals that are now flowing easily.

You can even elevate this to a level where you begin to feel great waves of happiness, joy and even euphoria! Imagine using this technique to promote well-being and even a natural high...which will enhance your life experience in so many ways...

Allow the client to enjoy feeling the positive responses they are eliciting.

And, even when you separate your fingertips, notice that the wonderful feelings linger. You feel great, pleased that you have learned a quick and easy way to feel good anytime, anywhere. You can now imagine some of those situations that in the past used to concern or stress you and how you can move forward knowing that you have the ability to choose how you are responding to any event, experience or person in a more helpful way.

Your creative, dynamic subconscious mind is already designing the ways that it will allow you to use all that you have learned in this experience to help you continue to improve in all ways...feeling good about yourself, good about your life...

Continue with any appropriate future pacing and suggestions. Following emerging from hypnosis, have the client use the finger-press anchor and notice how easy it is to feel good, once again encouraging them to use it often in the days to come.

Mini-Break for Weight Loss © Kelley T. Woods 2017

I wrote this for an audio recording to share for clients who live busy lives. Most people can find 10 minutes or so to listen during their day.

Begin by giving yourself permission to take a short recess. Take a nice, deep breath...hold it...and now release it.... continue breathing slowly now...and Let yourself now imagine being in a private space of your own...and turning your attention inward...to the feel of your heartbeat, to the sensation of your breathing.

As you begin to focus on your breathing, pay attention to how it feels to breathe in gently, taking in a sense of comfort and energy and then, breathe out easily, releasing any tension or worries...

Any outside distractions and sounds fade away as you begin to think about how wonderful you can feel...perhaps you are aware of a gradual wave of comfort that is starting at the crown of your head and now flowing downward through your body...relaxing and easing any stress or tension away...

In a moment, I'm going to count from 1 to 5 and as I do so...let your thoughts drift to a pleasant memory or place...bring up all of the details of being there in your mind's eye...see the colors, the scenery, hear any sounds, smell any aromas...and when I reach the count of 5, left yourself step right into this wonderful experience as your mind-body remembers how to feel so serene, so comfortable...

Here we go....1...double your relaxation...2...with each breath feeling yourself sink further...3...that's right...4...feeling even better now...nearly there.....5.

Notice how calm, how at peace, how content you are feeling. Isn't that wonderful?

Realize that you can enhance this feeling even more by breathing deeply and allowing yourself to engage even more with your perfect place...Relax even further...

And as you do so, let your thoughts focus on your desire to change your physical body, on your desire to release that excess weight...for all of your own, very sound reasons...

You are now in control...in control of your eating...in control of the way you are living your life...you notice that if any nervous tension enters your mind or your body, that you automatically breathe it away...pressing your fingertips together to join your calming breath in releasing that tension...easily...naturally...quickly....relaxing your way into this healthy new chapter of your life...

Whenever the thought of eating comes to mind, you find yourself looking down, to the right, and asking yourself, "What is it that I am really hungry for?" And if the answer you hear is not for food, you will be able to address that emotional hunger because you have all of the wisdom and resources within you to deal the feelings you need to deal with...from your enhanced state of mind...

And if you are in fact hungry for food, you find it easy to desire healthy, delicious and nutritious food...you enjoy eating like a gourmet...consuming your food visually, appreciating the colors and textures, the aromas...you feel compelled to always be seated comfortably, giving your whole undivided attention to your meal...you are taking your time eating...putting down your utensils between bites...chewing slowly...allowing the digestive juices to do their job...staying calm and relaxed while you eat...

And you are eating less...less often...many times, you cannot even finish the meal...you find you are quickly satisfied...feeling full...less is enough for you...less is plenty... eating slowly...in fact, you enjoy being the last one to finish your eating...taking your time, paying full attention to your meal and eating less...

And as you do eat less, your body is releasing that excess weight...naturally and safely returning you to your ideal size...bring that image of your healthier self to mind right now...let it appear in the center of your field of vision and welcome them...that's right...Notice how healthy and happy they are! You can't wait to reveal this version of yourself and you are doing everything in your power to allow this to happen...

You find that you love the way your body moves...whenever you are moving your body, burning away that excess weight, you feel great! Each and every time you stretch and walk or otherwise exercise your body you are leaving behind this old chapter of your life and stepping further into your wonderful, healthy, exciting, slimmer life...You notice that the more often you move your body, the faster this transformation happens and the faster the transformation, the more wonderful you feel...you love the way your body moves...

You are in control...you have made the best decision, for you, to let go of all of those outdated, unwanted negative feelings and along with them, you are letting go of that excess weight. You just don't need it anymore. It served its purpose and now it can leave...See and feel yourself, right now, breathing that weight away...that's right...doesn't that feel good?

And you can do this throughout your day; breathing any tension, along with that weight, away...living your life in a calm and content state of being...letting go of negativity and embracing happiness and joy...because you deserve it...you are a kind a loving person and now, you are being kind and loving to you...

(Emerge when ready with preferred method.)

Let it Go Weight Loss Script   © Kelley T. Woods 2017

This generic script is suitable for use within your session, following foundational work, but makes for a good recording to provide the repetition needed for habit change. Customization will, of course, optimize it for your client!

Following induction of choice:

> *I'll let you enjoy these moments of comfort and peace. Feel yourself just drifting down deeper and deeper with every breath as you sink further into trance and my voice goes with you. Perhaps you can imagine yourself in a favorite place and you breathe and look around, appreciating what it is that makes this place so special, so peaceful to you. Using all of your senses, enjoy the sights, the sounds, the aromas, touch whatever you wish to...Just luxuriate in this place of relaxation as you drift peacefully...breathing calmly....*

> *I wonder if you can imagine...as you drift here in this wonderful place, that tomorrow you will wake up and all of your concerns about your life, about your physical and emotional selves, are relieved. What will it be like to know that you have finally solved these issues? Can you imagine what that will feel like? I can tell you now...without hesitation...that you have already begun your successful journey to that state.*

> *Now...reach into your memories...and recall some of your past successes...Think about the times in your life when you have achieved victory over challenges...times when you were proud of yourself...times when you knew that you were really on the right track....Let that proud feeling well up in you right now and glory in that sense of pride...of accomplishment ...remind yourself that you can achieve anything that you desire...and remind yourself also that the main component to success is staying on the path....take a moment to recall those accomplishments and memorize these feelings of success....*

Pause

Now, let us address the subject at hand...that being the struggle with eating habits. As you continue forward along the path to success in your weight loss journey, you are discovering a variety of influences...and triggers that affect your weight and your health. Your life to this point has consisted of many different people and experiences, each of which have left a variety of imprints and impressions...some helpful...some not so helpful. And your inner mind has accepted some of these imprints and impressions while rejecting others, all in the pursuit of making you happy and healthy.

So think back now on some of these people, some of these experiences...that have and may still be influencing your attitudes and beliefs about food and drink and weight and health...Consider which of these are outdated...and no longer suit you or your current life goals. Perhaps there are some put upon you by others for their own reasons. If so, you can now acknowledge that you are the one who is truly in control of not only your thoughts but your actions. It is now time to take control of yourself, deciding that you choose to care for your body...you choose to improve your health by eating in ways that allow you to release the unnecessary, unwanted excess weight.

There may have been a time in your life when eating improperly was somehow a helpful thing to do, but that was then...and this is now. You now thoroughly and deeply understand and accept how important it is...how vital it is...that you get your eating habits under your control. Yes, you are taking back control. See and imagine yourself doing that right now...in this very moment...you are now in control of your own thoughts, actions and reactions when it comes to eating choices and indeed all choices in your life.

Because of this, you now understand the difference between a healthy hunger for food and an emotional hunger. Think about times and places when you might feel that you are hungry...

And notice how easy it is to look down and ask yourself, "What am I really hungry for?" And if the answer is not actually for food, but for some emotional need...such as peace of mind, or company, or entertainment...notice that you are able to fill that need in a reasonable and healthy way. You have all the wisdom and knowledge to know exactly how to satisfy that emotion without resorting to inappropriate eating because you are now freeing yourself from being a slave to emotional eating.

If, when you look down and ask yourself, "What am I really hungry for?" and the answer is for food, for energy for your body, you will look back up and think of an appealing, healthy food choice in just the right quantity. And when you prepare to eat, you always relax. You sit down and you relax, giving your full attention to your meal or snack. Before you begin to eat, you enjoy your food visually, noticing the presentation, the colors and textures, any aromas. You breathe deeply...in and out...and you relax.

You find it natural to eat slowly...chewing your food thoroughly...you have all the time you need to enjoy your food. Eating is a pleasant activity and when you eat slowly, you find it very easy to stop eating when you are full...even before all your food has been eaten...you can leave some food on your plate...you eat only when you are hungry for food and you find that you become full much sooner...less is more because you are in control...and because you are in total control slowly, but steadily, you are losing weight because you are in control...you will reach your ideal weight and be even more happy and more comfortable...and...you will find it easy to maintain your healthy weight...

198

And if, for any reason, you feel a craving for some unhealthy food you will hear your own voice, deep within you, saying "Stop! I'd rather be healthy..." You simply counter that craving with a long, deep inhale and as you exhale, you feel relaxed and any feeling of hunger reduces...dissipates...as your confidence and comfort increases proportionately. Your immediate response is to occupy yourself with some other, positive thought or activity...(insert specific alternatives)

Pause

Imagine yourself now, taking the time to enjoy preparing your food in advance. Perhaps you see yourself in the grocery store, shopping for amazing ingredients...you are having fun selecting the fruits and vegetables...some lean proteins... healthy fats...And isn't it interesting how those old, processed and refined foods have lost their appeal? They look to you almost like they have lost their color, their taste, their smell... you are attracted to those beautiful, colorful healthier foods ...and they are magnetized to you!

You are making the time and taking the time to prepare food in advance...you understand the value of always having healthy choices available and spending some time each week in this way insures your success. More and more, you enjoy this activity as a creative investment in your self-improvement journey.

Pause

Now imagine yourself as you wish to be...with the excess weight now gone...and wherever you are, notice how wonderful you feel...how healthy and strong...your clothing fits so beautifully, so comfortably...you did it! Notice how much more comfortable your entire body is now...You decided to release that extra weight and you did it...and it seemed effortless...you wanted to lose the weight and so you changed your habits and the weight just left...easily...naturally...See and feel how marvelous life is, now that you have taken control of your eating...that's right...

Pause

Let yourself now think about your physical activities...maybe you are going for a walk, or perhaps you are doing some other exercise, giving yourself a wonderful recess during your day...see how easy it is to enjoy this time... You even find yourself smiling and thinking, "I love the way my body moves!" Engaging in this activity or any other helpful physical movement is something that you look forward to and you realize that each time you do take a walk you are leaving more of the weight behind...just moving forward and entering this new, happier and healthier chapter of your life.

Pause

And you are taking time, during your day, to just breathe and release any tension or stress. Even if it just for a few moments, as you go about your chores or prepare to enjoy a healthy meal, you take a deep breath or two and let yourself feel wonderful...you are wonderful!

It is so wonderful that you know you are ready to lose that unwanted weight...and that you are doing it now...finding it easier and easier to eat healthy food in small portions...eating only when you are hungry for food...and stopping when you are no longer hungry.

And because of this, that excess weight is reducing... releasing...you are letting go of it...ounce by ounce, pound by pound...until you reach your ideal weight...your ideal, healthy and comfortable size. It feels so good to let it go...With each and every day, your confidence in your own mind's ability to help you grows stronger and stronger as all aspects of your improving life steadily respond in fantastic ways...

You are a kind and loving person and you are being kind and loving to yourself, easily finding new and interesting ways to care for yourself...and as you let go of the unwanted weight, you gain rewarding experiences, people and insights... steadily growing stronger as a happy and healthy person... relaxing your way into this new, lighter, more comfortable, energized life. And periodically, during your day, you remember to take a deep breath or two...as you exhale, you think to yourself, "Let it go...let it go..."

Float to Sleep Script   © Kelley T. Woods 2017

This hypnosis script is designed to incite the relaxation response, reduce pain and promote sleep. For my recording, I used Dan Kern's Isochronic Ocean backtracking, which clients greatly enjoy. It is best recorded with long pauses, allowing plenty of time for the listener to absorb and notice the shifts that occur.

You can use any of a number of progressive, relaxing inductions. I typically use an autogenic training process as it will quickly address any possible tension or discomfort. Continue with:

And as you lie there...relaxed...breathing gently in and out...nothing to think about...nothing to do...just letting go...with that lovely feeling of heaviness in your arms and legs...as if they are comfortably sinking down...and then a feeling of floating...that is safe and secure...as if you were sinking down and down...totally relaxed...just letting go... allowing your thoughts to drift away...nothing to do...nothing to think about...this is your time...and you have all of the time in the world...

just enjoying that relaxation...and as you relax each and every breath relaxes you even more...as your mind drifts deeper...and you can enjoy this natural and wonderful feeling of drifting down...and across...time and space...feeling weightless...and timeless...

Pause [cue background music]

and maybe you can imagine an island...far away... summery ...warm...soft light...gentle breeze...

and there is the scent of the sea...and maybe an aroma of spices and exotic fruits...

Feel yourself wandering here now...strolling along the shore...as you enjoy the texture of the fine sand beneath your feet and the caress of the warm water on your toes...

The soft breeze stirs your hair...and you breathe in the salty air...a deep, and complete sense of peace and calm is now coming into your body and mind as you drift naturally here in this marvelous place...

The iridescent shades of blues and greens in the water are so captivating...and relaxing...and the purest shade of blue radiates upward from the sea...filling the expanse of sky ...and far off...over the horizon...puffy white clouds float easily...and you float along easily, too...moving along that shoreline with ease and comfort...each step bringing you further into the deepest sense of relaxation that you have known in a long, long time.

And eventually, you decide to venture into that warm and brilliant ocean...moving slowly into the waters...submerging your feet and ankles...the warm, gently moving water massages and relaxes each and every muscle and tendon...you go deeper, allowing this comforting sensation to travel up and around and through your calves and shins...and deeper still, around your knees...

This gentle and relaxing water moves deeper still, with the perfect temperature for you, encompassing and caressing your thighs...your hips...removing any tension or tightness...each and every muscle and joint becoming loose, limp, and relaxed...

And now this beautiful water is moving up your torso, your chest, your ribs, circling your spine, between your shoulder blades...its magical touch is reaching deep within you to calm your internal organs....and you lie back...allowing yourself to float...feeling the water support you as it continues to ease and relax your arms, your hands...now your shoulders and moving up your neck...easily, soothingly...even the back of your head and your entire scalp is now relaxing...all tension leaves your face, your jaw...as you float there and feel the gentle warmth of the sunlight on your skin...

Pause

You notice that as you breathe, the sea breathes with you...and you move together with a soft and gentle motion...and you feel so safe...so secure...here in your ocean bed of comfort...

Perhaps you can feel how perfectly soft and warm your hands and arm feel right now...in this healing water...and your feet...your legs...suspended...yet supported...so relaxed...so absolutely comfortable...

And feeling the movement of the sea beneath you and all around you...flowing gently...up and down or maybe back and forth, with your breathing...you can float here...in total comfort...and you can let your thoughts drift away to whatever notion or idea you choose...while your body continues to relax even more...and when your body relaxes in this manner...

it's so easy to begin to let your mind relax, too...it's easy to understand the value of letting go...of giving yourself permission of experiencing this wonderful sensation of being rocked gently...

Pause

And maybe now, it's almost like you are on a boat...that's safely anchored near the shore...and you can feel the gently swaying of the water beneath you while you are secure on this boat...cuddled and wrapped in a cozy space...I don't know if you can smell the aroma of the wood of the hull or perhaps you notice the fresh scent of the linens of your bunk...but what you do notice is how relaxed, how drowsy you are right now, right here...in this place...this perfect berth on the sea... rocking gently...allowing the earth's waters to lull you away...

and you could remember an image from this experience...or a sound...or a particular feeling you enjoy...or you might recall something different to remind you...

and when you bring this to mind...you will recall this wonderful relaxed feeling...every time...your body will relax...your mind will relax...for as long as you want...a moment or an hour...you can choose to slip into this beautiful state of comfort...mind and body...whenever you need to...

all you need to do now is to choose...to drift away and rest even further or gradually come back...it's all up to you...

The Protective Shield for Perspective Shifts
© Kelley T. Woods 2017

I employ this technique when a client reveals discomfort around others or an inability to deal with perceived verbal or emotional attacks. It is also helpful for establishing boundaries not just for interpersonal relationships but for gaining autonomy over eating, drinking and other habits.

This is a Mindful Hypnosis approach, interactive and instructive in nature, so memory of the experience is desired. I use a conversational style and by merely having the client recall a past negative experience, they are already stepping into hypnotic engagement.

Now, you have previously described how it makes you feel (use client's words regarding feelings) *when you are around* (specific person or situation). *I am going to teach you how you can feel better about this type of situation with a powerful and easy tool. Does this sound desirable to you?*

Please close your eyes and think about the feelings that you have described to me, the feelings that arise in you when you are in this situation...put yourself back in time to that same place (list details) *by following the physical sensations that you are now feeling in your body. You told me that when you are near* (specific person), *you feel* (list the physical reactions)...

now let those sensations get a bit bigger right now so that you can really feel where they are and how strong they are...that's right...very good.

And let me know when you are right back there in that situation, with (person)...*Very good...and now you feel those feelings quite strongly, don't you? Yes, and I can see that you are feeling this way because I notice the changes that have occurred in your body when you are there with* (person)...

Repeat the reactions the client has previously cited.

Now, go to the beginning of this event, the beginning of your interaction with (person) *and, imagine the scene as if it's a movie and it's on pause, stopped at the beginning.*

Here, I am now handing you a remote control; you are the one in control of your movie. When I say to, you will push the Play button and the movie will unfold. I will ask you to describe what is happening in detail so that I may better understand your feelings and experiences.

Before we begin, are you watching the movie from a 3rd person vantage point, or are you actually in the movie, seeing it through your own eye viewpoint?

Depending on the answer, move the client into the 1st person position.

So here we go...let yourself push the Play button and have the movie begin...Tell me what you are noticing.

Allow client to experience the event all the way to end, prompting with questions such as, "*Now what are you doing?*" "*And what else is happening?*", etc.

When the end of the event is reached, calibrate the level of emotional tension and discomfort by asking the client where on a scale of 1-10 she feels the discomfort, having her consider the physical and emotional responses. Repeat that number back to her:

Okay...so you are feeling a 7 on the scale right now, is that right?

Now comes the fun part! Tell the client to rewind the movie and keep it in the Pause mode.

Take a deep, cleansing breath, and with it, release all of those negative feelings and emotions that are in you. Continue breathing as you clear your mind and let those just float away, you don't need them anymore...that's very good...Let me know when they have left and you are now feeling loose, limp, and relaxed...

Or any other patter you use for enhancing relaxation...

Now, imagine that you are surrounding by a protective shield. This shield is a sphere that completely protects you; it is opaque or maybe even translucent...It is now present, hovering within 18 inches or so...all around your body and you can breathe comfortably within it. Take some time to decide what it feels and looks like: it may be of a hard material or it may be supple, or even rubbery...it may have a slight tint of color to it...it may even have a temperature to it...that's entirely up to you...this is your own special shield...it belongs to you and it protects you.

An amazing thing that I will tell you about this shield is that it protects you from any negative attacks...whether they are verbal or silent...if they consist of an expression or a gesture...or even the negative energy that some people project...all of these will just bounce off of the outside of your shield...easily deflected without you even having to think about it.

The other really amazing thing about this shield is that it operates like a two-way mirror, in that while negative thoughts and words from others cannot penetrate it, you can send out any thoughts and feelings that you wish...isn't that interesting? Now, go ahead and add any more details that you wish to your shield...take as long as you like...

Allow some time for the client to design the sub-modalities of the shield.

Do you have your shield installed now? Good...why don't you see what it feels like to let that shield grow larger...let it now extend out to the edges of the room...how does that feel?... good...now, pull it back in close again...

Okay, now we are ready. You are still holding that remote control, aren't you? I bet you are wondering how it will be to go through that event again, this time with your protective shield fully installed...when I tell you to, push the Play button and we will do just that...you have your shield installed now...go ahead and push Play.

Allow the client to revisit the event quietly for a while...then ask,

"How is that feeling"..."What are you noticing?"

The client will usually state that they feels no emotional response to the previously negative energy. Often, if the attack is verbal, the words are muffled or even gone. The client may even notice that the scene is a bit hazy, although they are well aware of what is there.

Generally, there is a sense of comfortable detachment from what is going on; be sure to let the client realize how comfortable they feel, taking note of the absence of those previous limiting, unhelpful reactions. You can use suggestions of staying calm, confident and clear in their protective shield.

Calibrate the level of discomfort, which should be gone at this time, reminding them that they were previously experiencing it at a 7 or whatever measurement was taken. Once this is acknowledged, often with amazement and relief, proceed to the final, powerful aspect of this technique:

And now you know how easy it is to protect yourself from (person), *or anyone or anything that previously bothered you. Isn't this wonderful? I'm so happy for you that you now have this great tool at your disposal. You are a perfect candidate for using hypnosis to help yourself! In fact, there is more to this protective shield than you realize and now I'm going to share it with you...*

You have told me that you notice how relaxed and comfortable you are now, despite the fact that (person) *is trying to push your buttons...but you're not reacting, are you? And because you are not having that automatic, negative emotional reaction, I wonder if you notice how easy it is to just step back right now and really look at* (person)*...Can you do that? Yes, of course you can...very good...Now, from your calm and detached point of view, tell me what you notice about* (person)*...what is going on with* (person)*?*

209

Allow the client to make some observations and discoveries about the antagonist's behavior and motivations...you can prompt with questions such as,

"And why do you think this person is behaving this way?"

Use the client's comments to clarify where certain emotions may be rooted, i.e. anger is sourced in pain and why does the client think the antagonist is hurting...

And now that you are seeing (person) *clearly, maybe even for the first time, from your new viewpoint and gaining a better understanding of what is going on with* (person), *how does this make you feel?*

Common replies will be of feelings of pity or empathy although if animosity is strong it may be entertainment or repulsion. However, any previous feelings of being victimized or persecuted will be diffused. Use this new resource state and the new, more helpful emotional reaction to build self-efficacy in the client.

And feeling this way, with compassion for (person), *you notice that* (person) *is hurting...Why do you think that is?*

Perhaps the client states that the antagonist is lonely, or in pain of some type.

If someone is hurting, what is one way that you would like to help them? Would sending out feelings and thoughts of love and kindness help someone who is in such a sad position? Would you like to do that and see how it feels?

Client may agree. If not, tell them that's fine, too and that they always has that option, depending on the situation. In fact, remind them that they have the wisdom and discretion to send out any positive feelings OR not to send out anything at all! In any case, they can proceed, feeling secure and in control.

If they do wish to express helpful feelings:

Go ahead now and send out those feelings to (person) right now...That's right, let those expressions of unconditional love project right out of yourself, through your shield into (person).

If appropriate, this is a good place to provide the act of forgiveness.

And, as you are doing this, notice how that is making (person) feel...That's nice, isn't it?...very good. And, of course, I want you to notice just how it is making you feel...how wonderful it makes your whole body and spirit feel to be sharing that much love and kindness with someone who really needs it. Notice how this simple action is actually helping you heal those hurt feelings from the past...that you are now letting them go...you don't need them anymore...they have served their purpose and you are now ready to embrace joy and happiness in your life...wonderful...I am so happy for you!

I often quote one of my favorite philosophers, Eknath Eswaran, who wrote in his book, *Conquest of Mind*: "I will not be a jukebox into which others put coins!" This idea empowers the client with the idea that she can choose the music she listens to, dances to...not someone else.

And you can keep this protective shield with you, and take it out whenever you need it...you are now forever changed and have taken back your own power...your power to choose which emotions you will have...what a fantastic gift you have given yourself and you can't wait to go out into the world and use it...congratulations to you!

You can move on to use some future progression to demonstrate how your client will use their protective shield to not only keep those negative triggers at bay, but change your client's perspective to enhance their understanding and responses to life.

Three Golden Rings   © 2017 Kelley T. Woods

Use this process to help a client take on specific characteristics or abilities from a desirable role model. When it comes to healthy lifestyles, the possibilities are unlimited. This is another Mindful Hypnosis approach, so a focused and relaxed state is all that is necessary for engagement.

Imagine someone whom you really admire, someone who excels and exemplifies success in living a healthy, balanced lifestyle; someone whom you wish to emulate. This person may be from the past, or in the present, or perhaps even from the future...but this person has traits that you admire and would like to have yourself.

Define to yourself now which these traits are in particular: are they physical strength, determination, dexterity, focus? Is it the way they are able to enjoy just the right amount of healthy food to maintain the body they choose? Identify the traits that make this person so admirable to you. Now see yourself asking to "borrow" these desired traits; this person gladly agrees to share these with you. Be sure to say, "Thank you!"

Now I want you to imagine yourself standing in your focused, calm place. Look down and notice that, about a foot in front of you, on the ground, lies a glowing, golden ring of light. When I count to One, see and feel yourself step into that ring. Ready? Here we go...One.

As you stand there, within that ring of golden light, you will notice that it is slowly beginning to move upwards, and as it does so, you feel some sensations in your feet and ankles...perhaps a bit of tingling or even a warming. It is a pleasant feeling and part of you knows what it is...as the ring continues coming up higher until it reaches your knee height...and you are excited as you now realize that that sensation is caused by those desired traits being infused...You can feel some of your selected model's wonderful skills and attributes joining your own inherent abilities, enhancing them even more.

Now that golden ring of light is hovering near your knees and you look forward a bit, noticing a second golden ring, one step away. Go ahead, on my count, and step into the second ring, bringing that first golden ring with you.

Here we go...Two.

And you notice that as you have stepped into the second ring of golden light, that it is joining the first, making twice the power, twice the light...and it is slowly moving upward now...bringing with it even more of your model's prowess and success to you...continuing to infuse you with a comfortable and pleasant sensation as it elevates up, past your thighs, past your pelvic area and your lower back...moving up smoothly, surrounding you with that wonderful glow...encompassing your hands and arms now, gliding up your torso until it comes to a hovering place at the top of your shoulders. You feel amazing, knowing that your model's abilities have been duplicated and instilled in YOU...And as you stand there, enjoying this feeling of power and belief in yourself...you notice one more golden ring in front of you.

Bringing all of the golden light that surrounds you, let yourself step forward now into this ring as I count....Three.

This final ring of golden light is now joining your other ones, tripling the light and power around you. Take a deep breath and enjoy the feeling as this last ring of light begins to rise up, around your neck, circling your head, making your transformation complete as it travels over the top of your head and unites you and your model's traits in one new and amazing self. You feel complete and confident...you look forward to the next opportunity to demonstrate your new mindset, skills and attributes.

213

And this feeling will stay with you for the rest of the day or even longer if you wish. And anytime you wish to have this feeling return, at this intensity, all you need do is take three steps forward, counting, with each step: One....Two....Three.

For best results, future pace the client being able to step into their new found frame. Practice this in and out of formal hypnosis until it happens automatically!

THE HUNGER SCALE

0	1	2	3	4	5	6	7	8	9	10
Empty	Ravenous	Over-Hungry	Hunger Pangs	Hunger Awakens	Neutral	Just Satisfied	Completely Satisfied	Full	Stuffed	Sick

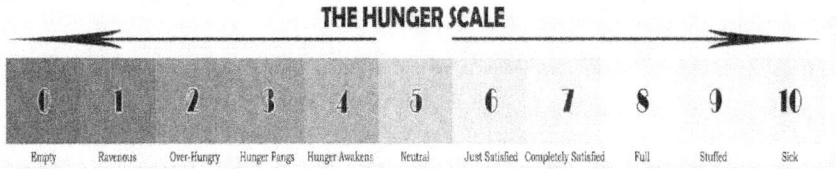

0-1 Starving State – I am so hungry I want to eat everything in sight. I feel urgency. I have severe hunger pangs. The feeling is intolerable. I may be shaky and lightheaded, weak, and/or sleepy. I am obsessing about food.

1-2 Ravenous State – I am overly hungry but not to the point where it is intolerable. I have pain in my stomach. I feel energy drained and a bit lethargic. I have lack of concentration and significant thoughts of food.

2-3 Solid Hunger State – I am solidly hungry. I have slight hunger pangs or twinges. The discomfort is mild. I definitely want to eat but I feel in control. I feel like I really know what I want to eat that will satisfy me.

3-4 Mild Hunger State – I am not quite hungry. I feel slight sensations in my stomach but I'm not quite ready to eat. I have a bit of stomach growling. Thoughts of food are mild. I know I will want to eat soon.

4-5 Neutral State – I feel neither hunger nor fullness. I really have no physical sensations at all. I have little or no thoughts of food. If I eat now, food may not taste as good as I hoped it would.

5-6 Mild Fullness State – I am a little full but I could eat a bit more to feel satisfied. I have slight sensations in my stomach but I feel it's too soon to stop eating. I'm beginning to feel a bit more energized.

6-7 Solid Fullness State – I am solidly full. I feel no hunger pangs. I feel slight sensations in my stomach but they are not painful. I feel satisfied and peaceful. I feel like I have some energy in my body. It is a good feeling. Food begins to be a bit less appealing.

7-8 Slightly Overfull State – I feel slightly overfull like perhaps I should have stopped eating a few bites sooner. My stomach feels like it may be distended a bit. I feel slight pressure on my stomach from my clothes.

8-9 Overfull State – I am overfull. I feel physically uncomfortable. My clothes feel tighter around my stomach. I feel drained and sleepy. I am bloated.

9-10 Stuffed State – I am exceedingly full. I feel extremely physically uncomfortable. Food no longer tastes good. I ate much more than I feel was good for my body. I have no energy. I feel like I could get physically ill.

215

Medical Professional Form

DATE

Dr.

Dear Dr.:

I am a Certified Hypnotherapist with a private practice in
_____. I am (list credentials and associations, if
applicable.)

Your patient,_____ , has requested help in the area of (issues).

As a hypnotherapist, my work involves helping my clients tap into their
subconscious abilities to motivate, focus on the positive, transform
unhealthy habits and living patterns, and remove limiting thoughts and
belief systems that keep them from enjoying full and satisfying lives. I
do not diagnose or prescribe, nor do I treat any physical or mental
ailment.

If you have no objections, please sign and date this letter below and
return it to me in the enclosed, self-addressed envelope. Please note on
the reverse side of this letter any limitations or anything else you want
me to be aware of, based on the medical concerns of your patient.

Thank you,

Your Signature

Doctor's Name

_____

Doctor's Signature

_____Date_____

Emotional Detox Technique

(from www.mindfulhypnosiscoach.com)

Use this "Make a Fist" technique and discover how easy it is to use this 3 to 5 minute exercise to release toxic emotions and feelings:

1. Close and open your eyes... Inhale and exhale deeply... Now create a safe space in your mind and allow yourself to feel whatever is disturbing or upsetting - get in touch with the feelings and as you do make a fist with your right hand, release the fist.

2. Inhale, and exhale deeply and close and open your eyes.

3. Now picture yourself in your mind as follows: You are having a great hair day; you are at your ideal weight; your skin is glowing with health; your eyes are sparkling with confidence, and there is a big smile on your face - because your heart is happy, your mind is peaceful and your spirit is playful. Excellent—now enjoy those feelings as you make a fist with your left hand and release it.

4. Now inhale and exhale deeply and gently close and open your eyes. Okay, now count to ten and at the count of ten; make a fist with both hands at the same time. Now just relax and mentally count to five before opening your fists...

Feeling better? Now try to get in touch with the unwanted emotions and feelings.... Amazing huh?

About the Author

Kelley T. Woods is a registered hypnotherapist in Washington State, in private practice since 2002. Helping clients not only with weight loss, but other chronic issues, she is the founder of Hypnotic Women, an online private international group of women who work professionally in hypnosis.

Kelley was awarded, along with her co-author Melissa Tiers, the 2017 Pen and Quill award by the International Medical and Dental Hypnosis Association for their best-selling book, *Integrative Hypnosis for Kids and Teens: Playing for Change.*

You can find out more about Kelley and her practice: woodshypnosis.com

Printed in Great Britain
by Amazon

78123865R00129